William J. Reynolds

Congregational Singing

D1489661

CONVENTION PRESS

Nashville, Tennessee
Church Services and Materials Division
5167-20

This book is a text for course 6720 in
Church Music Leadership in
the Church Study Course

Dewey Decimal classification number: 264.2
Printed in the United States of America

How to Use This Book

This book is designed to help those who are responsible for planning, directing, and accompanying congregational singing.

It is suggested that *Baptist Hymnal,* 1975 be used as a primary resource in the study of this text. Music examples included in the text all relate to that edition of the hymnal.

If the book is used as a text for group study, individual assignments may include:

Planning for worship services
The use of *Baptist Hymnal,* 1975
Selection of hymns
Organ registrations
Analyses of hymn texts
Rhythmic problems in congregational singing
Determinations of proper tempos

The appendixes are intended to be used as resource material for leaders of worship services.

Contents

Chapter 1

THE PRACTICE OF CONGREGATIONAL SINGING

Hymn singing can be a thrilling experience for a church congregation. I can recall occasions across the years when the excitement of the moment, the familiarity of the hymn, the acoustical factors of the room, the instrumental sound supporting the singing—all resulted in a memorable experience. Usually the hymn singing at conventions, evangelistic conferences, summer assemblies, and other such meetings produces a thrilling sound. But the singing of the local congregation Sunday by Sunday is the concern of this study. Hymn singing can be great for the local congregation; and the vibrant sound of the congregation singing songs of praise and testimony can do great things for the spirit of the church. Ministers and laymen throughout the world witness to this.

To the church in Corinth, Paul the apostle wrote, "I will sing with the spirit, I will sing with the understanding also." 1 Cor. 14:15. He is saying that the singing should be spirit-filled and that the singing should be understood by the singer. Singing is a spiritual experience, and it is an experience that is mentally perceived. Christian song is the overflow of the Christian heart. If the heart is full, the singing will be full. Louis F. Benson refers to Christian song as a "spiritual gift which each Christian brings to the sanctuary and contributes to a common song of spiritual fellowship."[1]

To the church at Colosse, Paul wrote:

"Let the word of Christ dwell in you richly in all wisdom; teaching and admonishing one another in psalms and hymns and spiritual songs, singing with grace in your hearts to the Lord.

And whatsoever ye do in word or deed, do all in the name of the Lord Jesus, giving thanks to God and the Father by him" (Col. 3:16-17).

With reference to this exhortation, Louis F. Benson comments:[1]

"Paul seems to see each singer apart, 'teaching and admonishing one another.' This is because Christian song is to him a purely spiritual function, the natural expression of a heart filled with the Spirit. In his concern that song should flourish among the Colossians he did not exhort them to form music classes but to deepen the spiritual life."[2]

Yes, spiritual values are involved in this experience, and the church's music leaders must positively claim the reality of this facet of congregational song.

The Congregation

In congregational services, the hymn singing is done by the congregation—all the people. This unsegregated, ungraded, unorganized body of people made up of some eager singers, some reluctant singers, and some nonsingers is the target group to involve, to persuade, to motivate in the singing experience.

The congregation is not a choir. To approach the singing of the hymns as a choral experience, using similar techniques regarding flexibility, tempo, dynamics, and interpretation, appropriate for a highly skilled forty-voice choral group, is to discourage many whose reflexive responses have been reduced by age or impairment. The singing of a hymn by a fine choral group and the singing of an average congregation are two different kinds of experiences. One is like the execution of a well-coached high school football team; the other like a touch football game played on the vacant corner lot by the neighborhood folks. In congregational singing, as in the neighborhood touch football game, anybody can

---

[1]Louis F. Benson, *The Hymnody of the Christian Church* (Richmond: John Knox Press, 1956), p. 44.
[2]*Ibid.*, p. 44.

play, regardless of age, sex, height, or weight. We use all available material.

The Difficulty of Explanation

Great congregational singing defies description. Other than employing such ambiguous words as "great, thrilling, tremendous, outstanding," what can you say? The fusing together of a text and a tune can result in an experience to the participant that is satisfying and rewarding in terms of personal pleasure. The factors that bring that about are difficult to verbalize. Can you identify the significant factors in the text or tune of "The Old Rugged Cross" that have made this song such a favorite in this century? By literary standards, the four stanzas would never be classed as great poetry, and the tune is rather difficult to sing. The rhythmic notation is awkward and jerky and most congregations make their own "homemade" adjustments each time they sing it. In spite of all this critical evaluation, when the text and tune are sung together, something indescribable happens that seems to speak to the masses of people. Again and again, this hymn will be found in the top titles of favorite hymn polls. How can we explain the magic of that hymn?

Or how does one explain the fact that "The Radiant Morn Hath Passed Away" (No. 32 in the *Baptist Hymnal,* 1956) was so rarely used in the churches that the Hymnal Committee for the *Baptist Hymnal,* 1975 voted against including it? Here is a hymn with outstanding credentials. The text is by Godfrey Thring, noted Anglican hymn writer, a co-author of "Crown Him with Many Crowns." The tune is credited to Charles François Gounod, one of the great nineteenth-century composers. Yet in spite of these credentials, the churches failed to sing it and its place in the new hymnal has been given to other material.

Subjective Influence

When judgment is expressed regarding individual hymns in our hymnal, we usually hear such well-worn phrases as "Oh, I like that" or "But that's not evangelistic!" or "That was my mother's favorite song and I like it." Objective, critical analysis is difficult to apply to our hymns. The association of hymns with experiences we have had is often a more significant factor than the value of the hymn content. To want to sing "When I Survey the Wondrous Cross" solely because it recalls the singing in a city-wide revival years ago or a statewide youth choir festival, or a favorite anthem arrangement learned at a choir workshop is to fail to grasp the strong commitment to Christ embodied in the text. Without a renewal of the commitment found in these stanzas, the singing of the hymn is meaningless.

Literary and Musical Values

Beyond the theological and doctrinal content of the hymn texts, there are literary and poetic values involved in hymns. Some hymn texts may be theologically and doctrinally sound, true to the Scriptures, and without error in Baptist beliefs. Yet, they may be of little or no value in congregational experience because of poor construction, weak vocabulary, awkwardness of meter and accent, and a total lack of poetic expression. Significant expression, words of strong meaning, ease of reading and ease of singing, lack of triteness, poetic structure that is perceived both visually and aurally—all these are positive factors for a hymn.

The hymn tune, to be a usable congregational song, must have musical worth. It must have a limited range (usually within the octave), it must be placed in a key which makes it lie in a comfortable range for singing, and it should contain no awkward leaps or skips. A singable tune is one so well constructed that it may be learned by the congregation without much effort.

Because of the musical and literary values involved, the material of congregational song is related to the arts. And this artistic experience is further compounded by aesthetic values, psychological responses, and physiological phenomena. All of these values, plus the spiritual values of the hymn singing should bear upon the individual in the congregational experience.

"When we sing, through our emotions the door of our understanding is opened to things beyond the meaning of words. We sing ourselves into the grace of believing; too often we talk ourselves into doubt. So then, let us once in a while be filled with the freedom and the ecstacy of singing. The reward will be great. It will be that we are numbered among the immortals who sing the never-beginning, the never-ending, the ever-old, the always-new song to the praise of God."[3]

The congregation may be totally unaware of the many facets of

[3]David McK. Williams, in an address cited by Armin Haeussler. *The Story of Our Hymns* (Saint Louis: Eden Publishing House, 1952), p. 6.

this experience when they sing a hymn, and music leaders in the churches are too frequently unaware of them. That helps to explain the difficulty in being precise, objective, and articulate in communicating with one another and with the congregation about congregational singing.

Teaching Congregational Singing Leaders

The inability to communicate clearly seems to exist also in the academic community where church music is a major program. Church music majors, whose vocational activity will involve a strong emphasis on congregational singing through their careers, receive little or no classroom instruction on this subject. A class in hymnology usually deals with the historical perspective of Christian song and most frequently from a literary perspective of the hymn text. Sometimes there will be a course offering in "Song Leading" but it rarely goes beyond the demonstration and physical practicing of hand-and-arm movements involved in the execution of traditional patterns for duple, triple, and quadruple groupings of accented and unaccented pulsations of the music. There is the implication to the student that if he can beat 4/4 and 3/4, he is a qualified leader of congregational singing.

The Need for More Resources

The difficulty in communication about and understanding of congregational singing is further compounded by the scarcity of helpful writings on the subject. Most of the resources classified in church and school libraries under "hymnology, hymnody, hymn singing," deal with the intrinsic content of hymnic repertoire. Furthermore, the most respected and scholarly writers, who are most articulate in extolling the glories and timelessness of the great classic hymns, usually become mute when trying to explain why "A Mighty Fortress Is Our God" (No. 37) and "All Creatures of Our God and King" (No. 9) never appear in listings of favorite hymns of the masses of the people. And, interestingly enough, those perennial favorites of the masses, "Amazing Grace! How Sweet the Sound," (No. 165), "In the Garden," (No. 428), and "The Old Rugged Cross" (No. 430) fail to make the pages of the scholarly writings.

Resources that deal with the practice of congregational singing, the mechanics of how it goes on, what happens to make the singing great, and what might be done to improve the situation when it is bad are sorely needed. These pages are designed to get to this matter, confront the problems encountered in the church, and seek solutions that might be helpful. The design of the material that follows was developed by participants in the Convocation on Congregational Singing in Nashville, Tennessee, April 29-May 1, 1974. More than two hundred church musicians were invited to share in the discussions, and many of the ideas and suggestions in the following chapters came out of those sessions.

Chapter 2

TEMPOS AND KEYS IN CONGREGATIONAL SINGING

A basic factor of congregational singing deals with tempo and key—the fastness and slowness, and the highness and lowness. The critical factor concerning tempo is to find that mysterious point on the metronomic scale at which the tune goes slowly enough to encourage everyone to sing along, but fast enough to provide a sense of aliveness and vibrancy. Relative to the matter of appropriate key, one must be found that will let all singers— high singers and low singers, together with that vast majority of medium singers—feel quite comfortable with the range of the tune.

Finding the Right Tempo

The choice of tempo for the singing of a hymn can greatly influence congregational participation. Only the familiarity or unfamiliarity of the hymn tune can be more influential in the singing of the people. A tempo that is too fast for the congregation discourages those who simply cannot keep up. They are aware that they are behind the tempo set by the leader and the instruments, and, rather than continuing to lag behind, they stop singing. The larger the congregation, the greater the problem of tempo. The "lag time" increases in direct proportion to the increased distance of the congregation from the leader, the choir, and the accompanying instruments.

7

A tempo that is too slow results in a plodding, deadly exercise for the congregation, regardless of the hymn. Vitality and excitement vanish as the tune plods from one note to another. Occasionally a gradual slowing of the tempo continues through several stanzas. By the final stanza the text and the tune seem literally to fall apart.

The individual who determines the tempo for a hymn should be aware of several factors that are critical in making the decision of how fast or how slow the tune should be sung.

1. *Textural factors*

(1) The style of the tune helps one to determine the appropriate tempo at which the tune should be sung. Each of the following styles seems to have its own tempo range: a chorale melody ("A Mighty Fortress Is Our God," *BH* 37; "Built on the Rock the Church Doth Stand," *BH* 35); a gospel song ("Jesus Is All the World to Me," *BH* 424; "He Lives," *BH* 438); a psalm tune ("All People That on Earth Do Dwell," *BH* 17; "Comfort, Comfort Ye My People," *BH* 77); a richly harmonized nineteenth-century English hymn tune ("The Church's One Foundation," *BH* 236; "Lead On, O King Eternal," *BH* 420); a rhythmic contemporary tune ("He's Everything to Me," *BH* 463, "Praise Him, O Praise Him," *BH* 18); a simple folk song ("Lord, I Want to Be a Christian," *BH* 322; "What Wondrous Love Is This," *BH* 106), a vibrant Sacred Harp tune ("I Know That My Redeemer Lives," *BH* 436; "Brethren, We Have Met to Worship," *BH* 260), a strong unison melody with sturdy keyboard accompaniment ("All Praise to Thee," *BH* 43; "All Creatures of Our God and King," *BH* 9).

(2) While it would be helpful to know something about the historical setting of each of these types of tunes, that knowledge is not essential to the joy of the singing. Inherent in each tune is a feeling of how the tune should go rightly, and it seems to "feel better" at that pace. The upright sturdiness of the rather "four-square" psalm tunes (DUNDEE *BH* 439; OLD 100TH, *BH* 6; OLD 134TH, *BH* 26; PSALM 42, *BH* 77; ST. ANNE, *BH* 223; ST. MAGNUS, *BH* 125; STUTTGART, *BH* 34; TALLIS' CANON, *BH* 443; TALLIS' ORDINAL, *BH* 402; TWENTY-FOURTH, *BH* 504) has a different "feel" from the joyful duple beat of "Jesus Is All the World to Me," *BH* 424. (See examples 1 and 2.)

(3) The drive of the melodic line can help in determining tempos. Tunes that are conjunct in profile, moving easily from note to note, can frequently be dealt with differently with regard

God Moves in a Mysterious Way 439

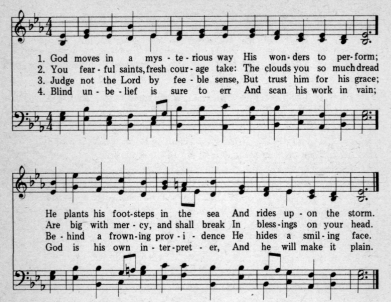

Words, William Cowper, 1774. Tune DUNDEE, *Scottish Psalter*, 1615. Alternate tune ST. ANNE, No. 223.

Example 1

Jesus Is All the World to Me   424

1. Je - sus is all the world to me, My life, my joy, my all;
2. Je - sus is all the world to me, My friend in tri - als sore;
3. Je - sus is all the world to me, And true to him I'll be;
4. Je - sus is all the world to me, I want no bet - ter friend;

He is my strength from day to day, With - out him I would fall:
I go to him for bless - ings, and He gives them o'er and o'er:
Oh, how could I this friend de - ny, When he's so true to me?
I trust him now, I'll trust him when Life's fleet - ing days shall end:

When I am sad, to him I go, No oth - er one can
He sends the sun - shine and the rain, He sends the har - vest's
Fol - low - ing him I know I'm right, He watch - es o'er me
Beau - ti - ful life with such a friend, Beau - ti - ful life that

cheer me so; When I am sad he makes me glad, He's my friend.
gold - en grain; Sun - shine and rain, har - vest of grain, He's my friend.
day and night; Fol - low - ing him by day and night, He's my friend.
has no end; E - ter - nal life, e - ter - nal joy, He's my friend.

Words and tune ELIZABETH, Will L. Thompson, 1904.

Example 2

to tempo than tunes that are disjunct or angular. Note the evenness in "O Master, Let Me Walk with Thee," *BH* 369; "So Let Our Lips and Lives Express," *BH* 456; or "Faith of Our Fathers," *BH* 143 as compared to the angularity of "Jesus Calls Us," *BH* 367; "Rejoice, the Lord Is King," *BH* 120; "Lead On, O King Eternal," *BH* 420, or "Angels from the Realms of Glory," *BH*, 87. Usually these angular melodies tend to move at a slightly slower pace because of the longer intervals involved. (See examples 3 and 4.)

Tunes that are more even may move a bit faster if other factors do not suggest a slower tempo.

(4) The length of the phrases to be sung—long or short—may influence the tempo. With longer phrases a slightly faster tempo may be desirable so that the congregation may sing the phrase in one breath instead of breaking the phrase into two or three "sub-phrases" in order to breathe. Here is a list of hymns with long phrases; the metrical measurement of the hymn is given also. (These numbers indicate the number of syllables in each line of each stanza.)

"Praise to the Lord, the Almighty," (14.14.4.7.8), *BH* 10
"How Firm a Foundation," (11.11.11.11.), *BH* 383
"To God Be the Glory," (11.11.11.11. with refrain) *BH* 33
"Hope of the World," (11.10.11.10), *BH* 364

Hymns with shorter phrases may be sung slightly slower, strengthening the meaning of the text to the congregation. Such hymns are:

"Have Thine Own Way, Lord," (5.4.5.4.D.), *BH* 349
"Fairest Lord Jesus," (5.6.8.5.5.8.), *BH* 48
"Break Thou the Bread of Life," (6.4.6.4.D.), *BH* 138
"No, Not Despairingly," (6.4.6.4.6.6.4), *BH* 173
"My Country, 'Tis of Thee," (6.6.4.6.6.6.4.), *BH* 511

(5) The character of the harmonic rhythm—the complexity or lack of complexity of harmonic change from one chord to another—affects tempo. In the first line of "Standing on the Promises," (*BH* 335), eleven syllables sung to eleven notes are all supported by tonic harmony. The fact that the B flat harmony is sustained through these two measures places no restraint or brake on the tempo (See example 5). However, "When Morning Gilds the Skies," (*BH* 44), with thirty-six syllables in a stanza, has forty harmonic changes in the tune. Only three times is the harmonic structure repeated between two consecutive beats. To move this tune at a fast pace violates the harmonic strength built

So Let Our Lips and Lives Express 456

1. So let our lips and lives express The holy gospel we profess; So let our works and virtues shine, To prove the doctrine all divine.

2. Thus shall we best proclaim abroad The honors of our Savior God; When his salvation reigns within, And grace subdues the pow'r of sin.

3. Our flesh and sense must be denied, Passion and envy, lust, and pride; While justice, temp'rance, truth, and love, Our inward piety approve.

4. Religion bears our spirits up, While we embrace that blessed hope, The bright appearance of the Lord; And faith stands leaning on his word.

Words, Isaac Watts, 1707. Tune WAREHAM, William Knapp, 1738.

Example 3

87   Angels, from the Realms of Glory

1. An - gels, from the realms of glo - ry, Wing your flight o'er
2. Shep - herds, in the fields a - bid - ing, Watch - ing o'er your
3. Sag - es, leave your con - tem - pla - tions, Bright - er vi - sions
4. Saints, be - fore the al - tar bend - ing, Watch - ing long in

all the earth; Ye who sang cre - a - tion's sto - ry,
flocks by night, God with man is now re - sid - ing,
beam a - far; Seek the great De - sire of na - tions,
hope and fear, Sud - den - ly the Lord, de - scend - ing,

Now pro - claim Mes - si - ah's birth: Come and wor - ship,
Yon - der shines the in - fant Light: Come and wor - ship,
Ye have seen the In - fant's star: Come and wor - ship,
In his tem - ple shall ap - pear: Come and wor - ship,

come and wor - ship, Wor - ship Christ, the new - born King!
come and wor - ship, Wor - ship Christ, the new - born King!
come and wor - ship, Wor - ship Christ, the new - born King!
come and wor - ship, Wor - ship Christ, the new - born King!

Words, James Montgomery, 1816. Tune REGENT SQUARE, Henry Smart, 1867.

Example 4

Standing on the Promises 335

1. Stand-ing on the prom-is-es of Christ my King, Thro' e - ter - nal a - ges
2. Stand-ing on the prom-is-es that can - not fail, When the howl-ing storms of
3. Stand-ing on the prom-is-es of Christ the Lord, Bound to him e - ter - nal -
4. Stand-ing on the prom-is-es I can - not fall, Lis - t'ning ev - 'ry mo-ment

let his prais - es ring; Glo - ry in the high-est, I will shout and sing,
doubt and fear as - sail, By the liv - ing word of God I shall pre - vail,
ly by love's strong cord, O - ver-com-ing dai - ly with the Spir-it's Sword,
to the Spir - it's call, Rest-ing in my Sav - ior as my all in all,

Standing on the promises of God. Stand - ing, stand - ing,
Standing on the promises, standing on the promises,

Standing on the prom-is-es of God my Sav - ior; Stand - ing,
Stand-ing on the prom-is - es,

stand - ing, I'm stand-ing on the prom- is - es of God.
stand-ing on the prom - is-es,

Words and tune PROMISES, R. Kelso Carter, 1886.

Example 5

When Morning Gilds the Skies 44

1. When morn - ing gilds the skies, My heart a - wak - ing cries,
2. The night be - comes as day, When from the heart we say,
3. Ye na - tions of man - kind, In this your con - cord find:
4. In heav'n's e - ter - nal bliss The love - liest strain is this,

May Je - sus Christ be praised! A - like at work and prayer,
May Je - sus Christ be praised! The pow'rs of dark - ness fear,
May Je - sus Christ be praised! Let all the earth a - round
May Je - sus Christ be praised! Let earth, and sea, and sky

To Je - sus I re - pair; May Je - sus Christ be praised.
When this sweet song they hear, May Je - sus Christ be praised.
Ring joy - ous with the sound: May Je - sus Christ be praised.
From depth to height re - ply, May Je - sus Christ be praised. A - MEN.

Words, *Katholiches Gesangbuch*, Wurzburg, 1828; translated, Edward Caswall, 1854. Tune LAUDES DOMINI, Joseph Barnby, 1868.

Example 6

into its musical fabric. The changing harmonic relationships pile upon each other too rapidly to be perceived clearly by the congregation (See example 6). This is purely a problem of musical construction and the difficulty some have experienced with this hymn may be attributed to a faster tempo that is appropriate.

2. *Rhythmic factors*

(1) The metrical rhythm will be determined by the leader at the time the hymn is sung. "How Firm a Foundation" (*BH* 383) will usually go at a slower tempo if it is sung four pulses to the measure. It will tend to move a bit faster if sung two pulses to the measure. Likewise, all hymn tunes in compound measure (6/8, 9/8, 12/8) will move slower with six, nine, or twelve pulses to the measure than if there are two, three, or four pulses per measure. The judgment of which should be used will rest on the leader and may change from one service to another depending on circumstances other than the rhythmic structure.

(2) Complex rhythmic patterns will cause the leader to sing at a slightly slower tempo to keep those patterns clear and distinct. Buryl Red's tune RAYMER for "For the Beauty of the Earth" (*BH* 49) seems to call for a slightly slower tempo than the familiar tune DIX (*BH* 54) used for the same text. When RAYMER is used, the tempo must be slow enough for the congregation to handle easily the subdivided quarter note beats. (See example 7) A faster tempo will tend to slur these rhythmic devices and the beauty of this compositional technique will be lost. Dotted rhythmic patterns and repeated (or "echo") lines found in such hymns as "I Will Sing the Wondrous Story" (*BH* 55), "I Will Sing of My Redeemer" (*BH* 465), and "I Know That My Redeemer Liveth" (*BH* 122), will make for a slightly slower tempo to keep from slurring these rhythmic patterns and the syllables of the words.

(3) The use of rubato—sections or phrases which the leader slows out of tempo—will tend to slow the overall tempo for the congregation. Some hymns frequently treated in this manner are "Softly and Tenderly, Jesus Is Calling" (*BH* 190), "O That Will Be Glory for Me" (*BH* 497), and "Make Me a Channel of Blessing" (*BH* 262).

(4) The use of *fermati* will tend to slow the tempo unless they are treated rhythmically, that is, given a specific time value. Such treatment keeps the rhythmic motion going and the congregation will sense that movement. For example, "A Mighty

49 For the Beauty of the Earth

Harmony

Christ our God, to thee we raise This our hymn of grate-ful praise.

Unison

1. For the beau-ty of the earth, For the glo-ry
2. For the won-der of each hour Of the day and
3. For the joy of hu-man love, Broth-er, sis-ter,

of the skies, For the love which from our birth O-ver
of the night, Hill and vale and tree and flow'r, Sun and
par-ent, child, Friends on earth, and friends a-bove, For all

and a-round us lies, O-ver and a-round us lies.
moon, and stars of light, Sun and moon, and stars of light.
gen-tle thoughts and mild, For all gen-tle thoughts and mild.

Words, Folliott S. Pierpoint, 1864. Tune RAYMER, Buryl Red, 1971. © Copyright 1971 Broadman Press.

Example 7

Fortress Is Our God" (*BH* 37) moves from phrase to phrase more easily if the quarter notes with *fermati* are treated as dotted half notes. These syllables and notes are thereby given three counts in tempo and the rhythm does not stop. The *fermati* in the first two measures of the refrain of "I Am Satisfied with Jesus" (*BH* 455) should be treated as dotted quarter notes, and the measures have the feeling of 5/4 in steady tempo.

    3. *Textual factors*

    (1) The mood of the text will influence the leader's judgment as to tempo. Hymns which express confession, repentance, humility, prayer, and other areas of quiet emotion will normally be sung at a slower tempo. Joyful, ecstatic expressions of the Christian life will generally be sung in a bit faster tempo. But this is not to imply that speed and ecstacy or excitement are synonymous. There are times and circumstances when it may be more exciting to slow the pace of a hymn tune carrying such a text.

    (2) The need for adequate time to articulate syllables will call for adjustment in tempo. Usually this problem is evident in longer phrases and/or repeated dotted rhythmic patterns. Some hymns which illustrate this are "Mine Eyes Have Seen the Glory" (*BH* 510), "Make Me a Blessing" (*BH* 290), and "Since Jesus Came into My Heart" (*BH* 487).

    4. *Other factors*

    (1) The acoustical characteristics of the room have some bearing on the tempo of singing. The acoustics (the reverberation factor) determines the duration of the sound after the release of phrases by singers and instruments, if the time duration is longer, each new phrase tends to "double back" on the phrase just concluded. All of this piling-up of sound tends to slightly restrain the tempo and pull it back.

    (2) The instrumental accompaniment and the skill of the players will affect tempo. If the playing is articulate and clean with distinct phrase endings, the tempo can move along steadily and in tempo. On the other hand, if the playing is sluggish, with continuous sound that provides no accent, the tempo will become unsteady and slackening and hearty congregational singing will be lost. (See the following chapter.)

    (3) The size of the congregation and its flexibility in responding to the leader of the singing and the sound of the accompanying instruments had an effect on tempo. Of course, the larger

the congregation the greater the problem of holding the group together in the singing. The smaller the congregation, the greater the flexibility in the singing. Of significance, too, is the sound of the accompanying instruments as perceived by the singing congregation. The volume of sound by the instruments must support adequately the sound of the congregation. If the level of instrumental sound is too low, no encouragement is given the congregation. (For more details see the following chapter.)

(4) The mood of the service influences the tempo. In a quieter midweek service, tempos seem to be slightly slower than on Sunday morning or Sunday evening when a larger congregation is singing. However, that is not *always* true.

(5) The time of day at which the service is scheduled affects the tempo. Tempos seem to be somewhat slower at early morning services than later morning or evening services.

(6) Familiarity or lack of familiarity with the tune to the congregation will affect the tempo. The familiar tune will be sung with a greater sense of confidence and sureness. Uncertainty and hesitancy will be evident in attempting an unfamiliar tune.

When the Tempo Is Too Slow or Too Fast

Congregational singing seems to be moving at too slow a tempo when the following symptoms are evidenced: (1) the singing loses vitality and the strength of accent is weakened; (2) the congregation is unable to complete phrases in one breath and the line of the phrase fades in the cadence, or end of the phrase; (3) the content of the text—the message of the hymn—loses its thrust in the increasing dullness of the singing; and (4) there is a decreasing participation on the part of the congregation.

Congregational singing seems to moving at too fast a tempo when the following symptoms are evidenced: (1) clear articulation of the text is difficult; (2) there is insufficient time to breathe between phrases; (3) the congregation has difficulty in staying together and two or three "tempo areas" may be isolated as each takes off at its own new tempo; and (4) there is a loss of meaning of the text in the hurried pace of the tune.

It is quite possible that there will be times when it will be most appropriate to make a change in tempo, increasing or decreasing it. The hymn may simply be moving too slowly or too fast and some corrective measure must be taken in midcourse. To accomplish this skillfully requires a high degree of communication and sensitivity between the music director and the accompanists. A change in pace must happen in a synchronized way. The music director cannot so effect such change without the immediate response of the accompanying instruments.

To be effective in tempo control, the organist and pianist need to develop skillful ways of making slight or, if needed, drastic changes in tempo by the keyboard technique they use. Staccato playing or sharply detached playing can serve as a brake to slow the pace, or as a sharp prod to move the tempo a bit faster. To play along in normal fashion will not be as effective in accomplishing these purposes.

Interludes between stanzas can be helpful in making tempo changes. For instance, on the last word of a third stanza the accompanist may begin a brief interlude increasing the volume of sound and establishing a *maestoso* feeling for the final stanza. Again, this must be done carefully and worked out in detail. Increasing use of this device (short of making it commonplace or routine) can become a joyful experience to the congregation, the music director, and the accompanist.

Suggested Tempos for Eleven Hymns

Prior to the Convocation on Congregational Singing the two hundred participants were asked to indicate the tempos they used in their churches for eleven hymns. The results of this survey were shared during the Convocation and discussed at length. The hymns were sung at the slowest and fastest tempos indicated in the survey, and a consensus was then sought as to the reasonable range in which an appropriate tempo would be found. The following listing shows the results of the survey and also the agreed upon range. The number given is the number of beat notes (quarter notes unless otherwise indicated) per minute.

	Slowest	Fastest	Reasonable Range
"A Mighty Fortress Is Our God" (*BH* 37)	44	114	80-90
"All Hail the Power of Jesus' Name" (*BH* 40)	80	126	94-104
"Amazing Grace! How Sweet the Sound" (*BH* 165)	60	120	80-92
"At Calvary" (*BH* 166)	80	126	100-112
"At the Cross" (*BH* 157)	62	126	90-100

"God of Grace and God of Glory" (*BH* 265)	72	124	85-96
"Holy, Holy, Holy" (*BH* 1)	72	132	90-100
"Just As I Am Without One Plea" (*BH* 187)	64	126	84-92
"Praise Him, Praise Him" (dotted quarters, *BH* 67)	60	118	75-84
"To God Be the Glory" (*BH* 33)	90	132	104-114
"When I Survey the Wondrous Cross" (*BH* 111) half notes	56	132	104-120

Significance of Keys in Congregational Singing

The key in which a hymn is sung is predetermined by the hymnal. The instruments normally play the tune in the key in which it is printed in the hymnal. However, there may be occasions when it is appropriate to raise or lower the key of the hymn tune. Any needed changes should be worked out well in advance of the service by the accompanist and leader of the singing to avoid any unfortunate misunderstandings. The following suggestions relate to possible key changes.

1. Raising the key one-half step on successive stanzas can add interest and variety. Be sure to start the hymn low enough so the final stanza is not too high. For example, sing the four stanzas of "O for a Thousand Tongues to Sing" (*BH* 69) in the keys F, Gb, G, Ab; (See example 8) "To God Be the Glory" (*BH* 33) in the keys of G, Ab, and A; "All Hail the Power of Jesus' Name" (*BH* 40) in the keys of F, Gb, G, Ab. The leader and accompanist must understand precisely how this will be done and how the key changes will occur. This should be rehearsed several times before the service. If the keyboard accompanist does not transpose easily, the tune should be written out in the needed keys. Also, the choir should be alerted to the key changes, and singing through the hymn in rehearsal will make for greater confidence all around.

2. Raising the key a half step on the final stanza can add vitality, excitement, and brightness. Such treatment of a final stanza brings a tremendous psychological "lift" the last time through the tune. This also needs to be well prepared and carefully executed.

3. Using lower keys in early morning services will greatly en-

Example 8

courage congregational participation. They can range from one-half to two steps down from the original key. Again, the writing out of the transpositions may be necessary. Written transpositions can be filed away for future use as, across the months, an increasing number of hymns may be sung in altered keys.

4. Key changes can be used effectively in a hymn medley—a series of tunes sung without interruption or interludes. The tunes can be arranged in order of ascending half steps:

"There Is a Fountain" (*BH* 107) Key of C
"Just When I Need Him Most" (*BH* 220) Key of Db
"Blessed Assurance" (*BH* 334) Key of D
"At the Cross" (*BH* 157) Key of Eb

In the final measure of "There Is a Fountain," the accompanist can play a C chord on the first two beats, then on the third beat play an Ab7 chord. (The pitch C is the common tone between the C chord and the Ab7 chord.) Begin singing "Just When I Need Him Most." In the final measure, play the Db chord, then the A7 chord to prepare for the key of D. At the conclusion of "Blessed Assurance" use the Bb7 chord to move into the key of Eb for "At the Cross." This is a very simple process of modulation.

Another way of doing this is through the use of the "circle of fifths" (the keys of C, F, Bb, Eb, Ab, etc., for example). In this process the final chord of the hymn just completed becomes the transitional chord by adding the minor seventh. Hence, C becomes C7 going to F; F becomes F7 going to Bb; Bb becomes Bb7 going to Eb; Eb becomes Eb7 going to Ab. Select appropriate hymns in these keys to make a logical sequence.

A third technique is that in which the accompanist devises improvisatory modulations appropriate to the keys of the hymns that the leader wishes to use in the medley. In this way there is no need for concern as in the sequence of key relationship. This procedure can be most interesting with a skillful accompanist. However, if there is not complete understanding between the music director and the accompanist in the move to each succeeding tune, a particular tune might begin in several keys at the same time. The classical musician would refer to this as polytonal music. The music director would refer to it as chaos.

Chapter 3

INSTRUMENTAL ACCOMPANIMENT
FOR CONGREGATIONAL SINGING

Instrumental accompaniment for congregational singing usually involves the organ and/or the piano. Other instruments may be used singly or in ensemble depending upon available resources. The effective use of instruments, not for "leading" the singing, but for accompanying it helpfully, is a major concern.

Several questions that relate to this primary subject call for consideration. Is there any difference in the role of the keyboard instruments in accompanying a choir anthem and a congregational hymn? What organ registration is most helpful in supporting congregational singing? How can the music director who has no organ-playing experience talk intelligently with the organist regarding registration for the hymns? Should the organist be the sole judge of appropriate registration? How can the organ provide rhythmic drive to help the congregation sing together? What effect does the lack of release in the organ sound at the phrase end or in the cadence have upon the singing? These are questions that must be confronted.

The Sound of the Instruments

Congregational singing involves human voices singing together. This singing can be to the accompaniment of musical instruments, or it may be unaccompanied. The sounds of accompanying instruments should enhance, enrich, and aid the singing voices, and be a part of the total ensemble. The instruments should not detract from the singing by calling attention to themselves. The instrumental sound should not overwhelm and engulf the singing and the singers, nor be so anemic as to be of little consequence.

The sound of the instruments should be in the same tempo as the singing, accompanying the congregational singing in the same way that accompaniment would be provided for the choir. The instruments should not run ahead or fall behind in tempo. Any attempt to "lead" the singing by being ahead any fraction of a beat greatly discourages the congregation. To find the tempo at which the congregation sings together—fast enough to have a sense of vitality but slow enough for everyone to keep up—is a most desirable goal.

The Introduction of the Tune

The playing of the introduction (giving out the tune) by the instrument has real purpose and reason. The introduction, if the entire tune is not played, should include the first and last line of the hymn. This provides a "mini" hymn tune that has some architectural structure and sounds complete. It reminds the singers of how the tune begins and comes to a musically satisfying conclusion. Suggestions for the introduction of the tune are indicated in the *Baptist Hymnal,* 1975 by the use of brackets above the tune. Usually this involves two pairs of brackets for completeness. At a glance the accompanist can know how much of the tune to play without having to make this determination uncertainly on the spur of the moment.

The introduction sets the tempo and establishes the key. The mood of the hymn is implied by the registration and style of playing. All of those things need to be clearly perceived by the congregation. Any variance in tempo during the introduction, any sudden change in dynamic levels, any sense of uncertainty confuses the congregation. In order to communicate these things clearly to the congregation, the accompanist must have a definite mental concept of them before the first sound begins. Such playing leaves no question in the minds of the congregation as to how fast or slow, how loud or soft, how boisterously or quietly, and at what pitch the tune is to be sung.

2 Come, Thou Almighty King

1. Come, thou Almighty King, Help us thy name to sing, Help us to praise: Father! all-glorious, O'er all victorious, Come, and reign over us, Ancient of Days.

2. Come, thou Incarnate Word, Gird on thy mighty sword, Our prayer attend! Come, and thy people bless, And give thy word success: Spirit of holiness, On us descend.

3. Come, Holy Comforter, Thy sacred witness bear In this glad hour! Thou, who almighty art, Now rule in ev'ry heart And ne'er from us depart, Spirit of pow'r.

4. To thee, great One in Three, The highest praises be, Hence evermore; Thy sov'reign majesty May we in glory see, And to eternity Love and adore. A-MEN.

Words, Anonymous, 1757. Tune ITALIAN HYMN, Felice de Giardini, 1769.

Example 9

Come, Thou Almighty King

Arranged by ALBERT L. TRAVIS

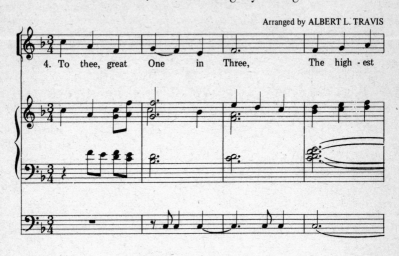

4. To thee, great One in Three, The high-est

prais - es   be,   Hence ev - er - more;

Example 10

Thy sov-'reign maj-es-ty May we in glo-ry see, And to e-ter-ni-ty Love and a-dore. A-men.

Style of Playing

Virtuosic playing with elaborate embellishment is inappropriate in a worship service. Particularly if the tune is a familiar one, the major contribution in instrumental accompaniment is for harmonic and rhythmic foundation. Providing this kind of support in the total ensemble sound makes for great singing by the congregation.

Free Accompaniments

The term "free accompaniment" refers to a harmonically unrestricted instrumental accompaniment for a hymn tune. The congregation sings in unison—everyone singing the melody—and the accompaniment is improvisational in character. That is, the harmonization differs from that given in the hymnal, yet is one that goes well with the melody. (See examples 9 and 10.) There are several excellent collections of free accompaniments available. (See appendix.) Sparingly used, they can bring excitement to congregational singing; too frequent a usage tends to make them commonplace. If they are used at the same place in the service each week, they become routine and ineffective.

Choir singers, organists, pianists, and musicians in the congregation are usually quite fond of free accompaniments. However, the average person in the congregation does not always share this interest. To him, the strange harmonizations are confusing and he has difficulty keeping the tune going. Free accompaniments usually are played at a higher level of volume and may prompt him to stop singing and listen. When that occurs, the beautiful and imaginative free accompaniment has provided discouragement rather than encouragement for hearty congregational song. To avoid such a reaction, the music director should provide some instructions to the congregation to let them know what is going on so they can enjoy the experience in a knowledgeable way. He might, for instance, ask them to sing the last stanza in unison, while the organist plays the free accompaniment.

The Use of the Organ

The Organist Edition of *Baptist Hymnal,* 1975, is published to provide the organist with the hymn tune printed as it should be played on the organ. The way the tune appears in the standard edition of the hymnal is for four-part or unison singing, and is not intended to be played in precisely this manner at either organ or piano. In other words, the hymnal version is vocal music, not instrumental music. Example 12 is the hymn "We Are Climbing Jacob's Ladder" as it appears in the hymnal. Example 11 is the same hymn from the Organist edition, and is designed for the organ keyboard. The notes to be played on the manuals and pedals are included on two staves. Note the indications for phrasing, the tying of notes together, and other notation changes to accomplish this purpose. There is no alteration of harmonic structure of the tune.

The most significant factors related to use of the organ for congregational singing are the sense of phrasing and the need for rhythmic playing. Too many organists play a hymn tune with continuous sound, the fingers keeping keys depressed all the time, causing some sound to continue without any break at all through an entire stanza, and sometimes through several stanzas. The fingers are not lifted from the keys at the ends of the phrases, nor is there any sense of rhythmic pulse. This style of playing may be employed at times when the organ is playing along, but does not give adequate support when the congregation is singing.

At the end of each phrase of the hymn tune, the organ should "breathe" with the congregation. The sound should be released at the instant the singing stops to allow for breathing, not after the inhalation has begun. When the people breathe, let the organ breathe also. When the moment of silence occurs, the organ should be silent also and should not sound over into the silence of the singers. The carryover of organ sound into the moment of breathing causes a tardy beginning of the next phrase by the congregation and thus contributes to a gradual slowing of the tune and decreasing of vitality.

The rhythmic pulse of congregational singing is the stabilizing factor in keeping the singing together. The band in the half-time show at the football game depends on the percussion section—not the brasses or woodwinds—to keep the band together as they march down the field and go through their drills. This is not to suggest that we need drums on Sunday morning to keep our singing together, but it is to suggest that rhythmic pulse is vital to congregational singing. There are ways to provide this with the accompanying instruments. In some hymns the pulse will be stronger and with greater accent than in other hymns. "All Hail the Power of Jesus' Name" (*BH* 40) and "We're Marching to

We Are Climbing Jacob's Ladder

1. We are climb - ing Ja - cob's lad - der, We are
2. Ev - 'ry round goes high - er, high - er, Ev - 'ry
3. Sin - ner, do you love my Je - sus? Sin - ner,
4. If you love him, why not serve him? If you

climb - ing Ja - cob's lad - der, We are climb - ing
round goes high - er, high - er, Ev - 'ry round goes
do you love my Je - sus? Sin - ner, do you
love him, why not serve him? If you love him,

Ja - cob's lad - der, Sol - diers of the cross.
high - er, high - er, Sol - diers of the cross.
love my Je - sus? Sol - diers of the cross.
why not serve him? Sol - diers of the cross.

Words and tune JACOB'S LADDER, Traditional Negro Spiritual.

Example 11

We Are Climbing Jacob's Ladder 147

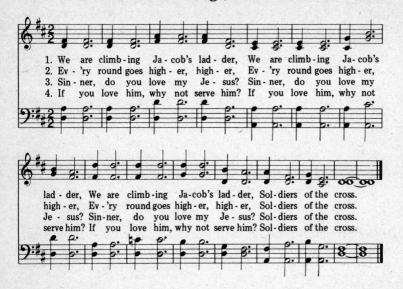

1. We are climb-ing Ja-cob's lad-der, We are climb-ing Ja-cob's
2. Ev-'ry round goes high-er, high-er, Ev-'ry round goes high-er,
3. Sin-ner, do you love my Je-sus? Sin-ner, do you love my
4. If you love him, why not serve him? If you love him, why not

lad-der, We are climb-ing Ja-cob's lad-der, Sol-diers of the cross.
high-er, Ev-'ry round goes high-er, high-er, Sol-diers of the cross.
Je-sus? Sin-ner, do you love my Je-sus? Sol-diers of the cross.
serve him? If you love him, why not serve him? Sol-diers of the cross.

Words and tune JACOB'S LADDER, Traditional Negro Spiritual.

Example 12

Zion" (BH 505), for example, will require a strong rhythmic pulse, while "Sweet, Sweet Spirit" (BH 255) and "Speak to My Heart" (BH 355) require much less strength in the rhythmic pulse felt by the congregation. At the same time, the pulse felt in all four should be regular and steady.

The only technique by which the organist can increase the strength of the pulse is by the contrast of sound and silence. Striking the key with great force or little force has no effect on the accent, for the pipes (or the speakers in an electronic organ) sound the same regardless of how hard the key is struck by the player. Legato playing provides less strength in the pulse, while staccato playing increases the pulse. Detached (or staccato) playing can provide strong rhythmic drive to move the congregation in the hymn singing and control the pace of the tune.

All the hymns in the hymnal are arranged for four-part singing, or for unison singing with keyboard accompaniment. "We Are Climbing Jacob's Ladder" (No. 147) example 12, is the way this spiritual appears in the hymnal and is written in musical notation for four voice parts—soprano, alto, tenor, and bass. This is intended for singing, but not for playing in exactly the same way. Example 11 is the same tune as it appears in the Organ edition of Baptist Hymnal. The notation of the melody is the same, but the other notes are not the same. Some repeated notes are tied—even tied across bar lines. The pedal notes are repeated across the measure bars to keep the rhythm moving. The "alto" notes are usually tied across measure bars because these are less significant rhythmically. The "tenor" notes are repeated with the melody to give support to the melodic line. Note the quarter rests indicated at the end of each phrase. These should be strictly observed and the sound released on the last half of the second beat of these measures.

The resources for registration will vary from one organ to another. Each organist should explore fully the resources of the instrument and utilize them fully. Using the same registration for all stanzas of all hymns becomes dull and unexciting to the congregation. The text of each stanza usually will provide some clue as to what the registration should be. Generally, the registration should be on the bright side, not thick and "tubby." The use of 8' pitch alone merely confronts the congregation with sounds at the same pitch they are singing. Stops of 4' and 2' pitch and mixtures can add color, brightness, and helpful sound. Remember that the texture of the sound is more important than the mass of volume.

There are too many variables involved in organ playing for congregational singing to permit dogmatism at this point—resources of the organ, registration, acoustical properties of the room, size of the congregation, etc. The way the organ is played is most significant. Recording the Sunday morning hymn singing from the back of the auditorium or the balcony can provide helpful insights for the music director and organist. A study of the tapes of the services reveal the degree to which the congregation, choir and instruments stay together, and will show the positive or negative aspects of the sound of the organ. If you make such a study, be sure to keep a record of organ registrations used on each hymn and on each stanza. You will need it to determine which registrations are effective and which ones come off poorly.

The Use of the Piano

The piano is a percussive instrument. Greater accent is achieved by striking the keys with greater strength. The rhythmic pulse of the hymn tune should be increased or decreased as required by the tune, the congregation, the acoustical properties of the room, and other factors affecting the singing. Organ sound is continuous in intensity and volume. When you depress the key, the pipes or speakers sound and continue sounding without change until the keys are released. The piano sound is deteriorating as long as the piano key remains depressed. The moment the key is struck is the moment of loudest sound. The deterioration begins at that moment and continues until the sound completely fades, or until the key is released and the string is damped. Renewing the sound requires that the key be struck again and again and again.

The most effective piano accompaniment for the congregational singing occurs when the pianist provides solid harmonic and rhythmic undergirding for the congregation. Unless the hymn tune is unfamiliar, melodic delineation is not significant, for the singers are not dependent on the piano to underline the melody. Hymn tunes of different characters, moods, and texture will be played in different ways by the pianist. For example, "Sweet Hour of Prayer," "All Creatures of Our God and King," "Be Thou My Vision" and "When We All Get to Heaven" would not be played in the same manner. It would be generally agreed, however, that inappropriate embellishments, excessive loud playing, and rhapsodic treatment of the tune are detrimental to congregational singing. Such practices are frequently attention-getting techniques which meet the ego needs of the pianist, but say to the congregation, "Don't pay any attention to what you are singing, just see what a great piano player I am!"

The Use of Keyboard Instruments

In Southern Baptist churches the general practice is to use both organ and piano for congregational singing. Some churches have only a piano. However, there are many churches that have both instruments but use only the organ. This is true usually where the sound of the organ and the skill of the organist are adequate for accompanying the congregation. The sound of an organ with adequate tonal resources will permeate the building in a manner that the piano cannot duplicate. In a church whose organ is not adequate and whose organist does not play skillfully, the sound of the piano is frequently added to reinforce the organ. There are also churches in which only the piano is used, either because it is the only instrument available, or because of the personal preference of the director or the congregation.

Since the instruments are accompanying and their major objective is assisting the congregation to sing together, each congregation or each music director will need to determine the best means to accomplish that objective.

Unaccompanied Singing

The occasional use of unaccompanied congregational singing can bring an experience of unusual significance. Unaccompanied singing frees the congregation from a dependence on the instruments. During the singing of a hymn with instruments, portions of individual stanzas or entire stanzas can be sung unaccompanied. No announcement or explanation to the congregation is necessary. If the organ sound gradually fades out during a stanza, the congregation will sense soon that the singing goes on without the instruments. This can happen on the second stanza, and after that stanza is completed, the third stanza can begin unaccompanied. Halfway through the third stanza, the instruments may begin playing unobtrusively and increase the level of sound to the end of the stanza. The fourth stanza then may be sung with full instruments. If you want to add variety to your congregational singing, try this formula.

When confidence on the part of the congregation has been built, an entire hymn may be sung unaccompanied. The need to establish the key may be accomplished by letting the organ or piano give out the tune and then play no further. If the song leader has a pleasant and steady voice, he or she may simply begin singing and the congregation will follow immediately. So sang our Baptist forefathers, and such practice used thoughtfully brings increased interest in congregational song.

Two words of caution. Do not attempt unaccompanied singing without planning and experience, and do not overuse it so that the too frequent use makes it commonplace.

The Use of Non-Keyboard Instruments

Instrumental ensembles made up of talented players from the church family can add brightness and joy to congregational singing. The sound of additional instruments should blend in with the singing and not overpower or overwhelm the congregation in such a manner as to discourage singing and encourage listening.

The Moravians and The Salvation Army each have a long history of using instruments to play hymn tunes and to accompany hymn singing. Those who have experienced these services know the strength of the instrumental sound.

Many uses can be made of an instrumental ensemble in hymn singing. The ensemble can give out the introduction to the hymn tune and then accompany the congregation. Some variety can be achieved by alternating stanzas with the ensemble and the piano and organ, and by the singing of unaccompanied stanzas. An interlude by the ensemble might be played between the third and fourth stanzas by repeating the final one or two phrases of the tune.

Handbell choirs can be used effectively with congregational singing. The handbells can play introductions and interludes between stanzas. An interlude may be a portion of the tune or the entire tune. If handbells are used during the hymn singing and the singing is full and hearty, the sound of the bells may be lost. Also, the handbells become a negative factor if the members of the congregation merely listen to the bells and do not sing.

Acoustic guitars amplified through a sound system that reproduces the guitar sound faithfully without distortion can accompany congregational singing. This sound goes better with quieter hymns of devotion or consecration such as "The Nail

Scarred Hand," (*BH* 192), "What Wondrous Love Is This," (*BH* 106), "Lord, I Want to Be a Christian," (*BH* 322), "Morning Has Broken," (*BH* 151).

The Autoharp may be used to accompany congregational singing as long as the harmonies of the hymn tune are within the capabilities of the instrument at hand, and if the congregation can hear the sound of the instrument. Careful amplification will be helpful in larger groups. The hymns mentioned earlier for use with guitar also work well with the Autoharp.

Rhythm sections—electric bass guitar, rhythm guitar, drum set, and piano—can be used in an exciting way through careful planning when the sound is appropriate to the hymn singing involved and to the congregation. Again, the sound must support congregational singing and must not attract attention to itself and become a performance for spectators. If you wish to use this instrumental sound in the service by itself, then make an appropriate place for it and let the people listen and share in a planned experience.

The Music Director and Instrumentalists

Congregational singing goes on at its best when there exists the finest relationship between the one responsible for the music and those who provide the instrumental skills. First, an understanding of the objective to be accomplished and the need for togetherness in the congregational singing is imperative. Such relationship and communication depend on spiritual maturity, mutual respect, and continual evaluation and sharing.

All the details of this experience need to be understood clearly. The congregation does not need to know all the specifics involved in hymn singing, but the leader and the instrumentalists must have no secrets from each other. Desired tempos, tempo changes within the hymn, changes in dynamic levels, modulations, going from one hymn to another in the same key or another key, the number of stanzas to be sung—all should be fully understood and rehearsed, if rehearsal is necessary. It is embarrassing to the leader, the instrumentalists, and the congregation when something "falls apart" due to lack of preparation.

The need for lowering or raising the key for a hymn should be communicated to the instrumentalists so that the new key can be written off on manuscript paper if transposition is not a ready skill.

The music director should know fully the skills and abilities of the instrumentalists, and should seek to utilize these skills to the fullest. He should also be acutely aware of their limitations and not expect the impossible. Do not blame a person for what he cannot do, cannot play, cannot sightread, or cannot execute related to congregational singing. The music director will wisely accept the circumstances in which he finds himself and use all available resources to the greatest benefit. Unkindness, impatience, hostility, harsh criticism, and the ultimate breakdown in communications will only increase the problems. The best of musicianship, dependability, flexibility, maturity, loyalty, cooperation and thoughtful concern are characteristics most needed in these relationships.

The Physical Location of the Instruments

The piano and the organ console should be placed so that the pianist and organist can hear the instruments and the congregational singing. This makes possible a much better control of the balance of sound. An unimpaired sight line between the organist and pianist and the music director is essential. Where problems of sight line exist and the instruments cannot be moved easily, the music director may solve the problem by moving his position forward, backward, or to the right or left.

Carpeting under a piano will absorb a quantity of sound, and some of the brightness of the sound will be lost. A solid railing panel around the piano will "box in" the sound. A grand piano contributes most effectively when the lid is opened toward the congregation. An upright piano should not be placed so that its sounding board (back side) is flat against a wall. It should be pulled away from the wall at an angle to the right or to the left to let the maximum sound out and also to give the pianist a better sight line to the music director.

It may be necessary in some churches, because of railings, carpet, location, or other factors to amplify the piano sound for congregational singing. A good system should be installed that will amplify the piano without distortion. The level of sound needs to be carefully set so that it carries well over the house system without blasting or distortion. Then, when the piano is playing alone at other times in the service, the volume level can be turned down completely. Only when the congregation is singing is reinforcement needed. Exceptions to this rule may arise when acoustical problems require constant amplification of the piano. The controlling principle is that the sound of the piano must never be distorted through amplification.

Chapter 4

PHYSICAL FACTORS INFLUENCING HYMN SINGING

Congregational singing is made up of facets of musical, spiritual, emotional, psychological, theological, poetic, aesthetic, and communicative significance. In addition to these, physical factors that we perceive aurally and visually, consciously or unconsciously, are related to congregational singing. The architectural design, the acoustics, the lighting, the temperature and humidity, the room dimensions, the wall, floor, and ceiling surfaces are matters of concern that can strengthen or weaken the effectiveness of the experience of congregational singing. This chapter will not be an attempt to deal extensively and technically with these physical factors, but they will be dealt with briefly.

Architectural Design

In an existing building those who are responsible for the congregational singing usually have little control over the physical factors, yet it will be helpful to identify them for increased awareness.

In the planning of a new building the general design takes shape in the mind of the architect. This design is accepted, adjusted, changed, modified, or rejected by a committee elected as representatives of the congregation. There are, of course, multiple needs to be met in the designing of the place where the congregation gathers to praise God and proclaim the gospel of Jesus

Christ. The congregational singing depends upon the hearty participation of all the people as they share together the joy of praise and fellowship. The visual images each person perceives—both objectively and subjectively—and the aural sensations which are received bear upon the value of this experience to the individual and the corporate experience to the whole congregation.

1. *Proportions of room dimensions.* The dimensions of the room—width, length, and height—can be properly balanced for the size of the congregation. A room that is too wide or too long is out of balance, and a sense of togetherness is difficult to achieve in the singing of the congregation. If the distance from floor to ceiling is too great in proportion to the rest of the room's dimensions, the sound of the singing may be dissipated and lost. If there is not sufficient height, the singing will be muffled and distorted.

2. *Seating design and arrangement.* The details of the design of seating—pew length, spacing of rows, and overall arrangement—should contribute to a spirit of unity and togetherness in the congregation. Balconies can be designed in such a way that those seated there feel themselves to be a part of, rather than apart from, those seated on the main floor level. In services when the building is only half full, the congregational singing will be better if the people sit close together. When they are scattered throughout the auditorium, the singing is usually poor. Back pews may be roped off and ushers can suggest that the people sit toward the front of the auditorium.

3. *Lighting.* There should be sufficient light for the congregation to read from the hymnal without strain or difficulty. Lighting should not exceed fifty candle feet nor should it be less than thirty candle feet. Fluorescent lighting is not usually recommended for congregational services.

In recent years more churches have provided for rheostat control making possible the dimming and brightening of lights and the individual control of lights in the room—overhead lights in sections, choir lights, pulpit spotlight, and other adjustable spotlights. Because the church is not a theater and the people in the congregation are not merely spectators, the rostrum and choirloft are not a stage and the worship leaders are not actors. The dimming of the "house lights" and the spotlighting of "action on the stage" is inappropriate. Those in the congregation are participants in worship and praise and testimony, and the lights should be bright enough to encourage their response. Dimming the house lights relegates the members of the congregation to the role of spectators, and does not encourage hearty participation in the hymn singing even if the lights are brought up full at that time. For services where dramatic presentations require complex light control, those facilities are most desirable and effective. But during the regular congregational services, all the participants—including those in the congregation—should be well lighted.

4. *Temperature and humidity control.* The comfort of the congregation relative to temperature and humidity affects congregational singing. The discomfort of being too hot or too cold will not be conducive to sharing in joyful song. In recent years, more churches have included in their building plans, or have added to existing buildings, equipment to give year-round temperature control. With the closed doors and windows of air conditioned churches, the sound of the singing of familiar hymns no longer can be heard by passersby. In rural areas, in churches lacking in these modern conveniences, the sound of the hymn singing still can be heard by those outside the building.

5. *Location of organ.* The placement of the sound source (pipes of a pipe organ or the speaker cabinets of an electronic organ) should be within the permanent walls of the room rather than in a separate isolated niche or chamber. Placing the pipes or speakers in a typical "organ chamber," which is more like another room attached to the auditorium with a small grill-covered opening into the auditorium, is to be avoided. This not only hides the pipes or speakers, but also hides much of the sound and brilliance. It is much more desirable to think of the sound source as being in the room with the congregation. With the moveability of electronic speakers, it is possible to experiment with different locations to seek the best placement for congregational singing.

The placement of the organ console (whether pipe or electronic) involves several considerations:

(a) The best location for the organist to hear the sound of the organ to properly balance the texture and volume of registration with the texture and volume of the sound of the singing.

(b) The best location for sight lines to the pastor, music director, and other persons or areas of activity which need to be observed—such as those collecting the offerings.

(c) The best location possible for sight lines and hearing of the piano in order that both instruments can be used effectively for accompanying the congregational singing.

(d) The best location regarding the overall design of the rostrum, choirloft, and piano and organ space within the limits of available space.

It has been the usual practice in recent years to place the organ console to the congregation's right. Other churches have made space in the center of the choir area in front of the choir. Others have compromised at some point between these two placements. When the console is placed too far to the congregation's right, the organist has difficulty in hearing the congregation, the choir, and soloists and in making any judgments regarding the balance of sound. Being too far to the right puts the organist in the "worst seat in the house" as far as the music is concerned.

6. *Location of the piano.* To be of the greatest assistance in congregational singing, the piano should not be enclosed in a piano stall. An upright piano should be placed so that its sounding board (the back side) is not pushed against a wall. To place an upright piano near a hard surface wall and at an angle to the wall will reflect the sound of the piano toward the congregation and give greater support for the singing. A grand piano is most effective when it is positioned so that the lid opens toward the congregation. The piano area should be large enough for a grand piano to be turned, with lid open, toward the congregation for hymn singing, and, at other times, be turned toward the choir to support choir singing. A grand piano truck (with large rubber rollers) will make this possible.

The pianist should be able to see the organist as well as hear the organ. The location of the organ console will affect the location of the piano. Both may be in the center area in front of the choir, or at points away from the center of the rostrum, the organ console to the right and the piano to the left.

Never place carpeting under a piano because of its sound absorption.

7. *Wall, floor, and ceiling surfaces.* When musical sound is produced by the congregation in hymn singing, or by the choir or the instruments, the church building becomes a musical instru-

ment. The sound takes the shape of the building. The characteristics of the sound are enriched and reinforced, or dulled and diminished by the surfaces of the walls, the floor and the ceiling. The same congregation, choir, or organ, will sound quite different in two different church buildings because of the difference in the wall, floor, and ceiling surfaces. This is known as the acoustical factor, the sum of the qualities that determine the value of an enclosure or a room as to distinct hearing.

The science of acoustics is complex and confusing to the laity. Disagreement is quite common among those who are supposed to be authorities in acoustical engineering. There are, however, some general areas of agreement that bear upon the sound of congregational singing. To attempt a technical treatise in this area goes beyond the scope of this book and the knowledge of this writer. However, it must be recognized that the reinforcement of the sound of congregational singing by the wall, floor, and ceiling surfaces is most desirable. Persons with no knowledge of acoustics can readily recognize whether or not the sound of congregational singing in a given room "feels good." If there is no reinforcement from the room, no reverberation factor, the singing will be dull, lifeless, and discouraging. Places of worship where walls, ceilings, and floors are covered partially or completely with highly absorbent materials have little possibility of producing exciting congregational singing.

With regard to the sound in the room, the floor is the greatest surface of absorption, the walls the greatest reflective surface, and the ceiling the greatest dispersion surface. Far greater sound absorption occurs with wall-to-wall carpeting than with aisle carpeting. In churches that have hard surfaces on the rostrum or platform areas those responsible for those sessions do not seem to regret that they did not carpet this area. The sound of both speech and music from the area is brighter and clearer if the surface is made of nonabsorbent material such as marble, synthetic marble, stone, asphalt, cork tile, wood, or some similar material.

Acoustically speaking, if the room is too "alive," there is too little absorption of sound, causing the sound to linger too long in the room, which blurs together indistinctly the words and the harmonic changes of the music. If the room is too "dead," there is too much absorption of sound and the sound dies instantly without any delay or reverberation. The difficulty encountered in acoustical design for churches is that of providing sufficient reverberation to reinforce the sound of congregational singing and at the same time, of making sure there is no difficulty in hearing the spoken word distinctly. A compromise that seems to be in the best interest of both music and speech places the range of the reverberation factor between 1.5 and 2.5 seconds. This means that the sound of congregational singing at any point will linger in the room (bouncing from wall to wall and floor to ceiling and all around) from one and one-half seconds to two and one-half seconds.

Where acoustical problems are identified in existing buildings, some effort should be made to improve or correct them. Technical advice should be sought to avoid expensive alterations that result in no improvement. It is often quite surprising how inexpensive adjustments or modifications can be made, greatly improving the sound of congregational singing.

8. *Sound Amplification System.* In relationship to congregational singing, mention is made of the use of some type of sound reproduction or amplification system to meet two possible needs:

(a) The need to amplify slightly the sound of the piano. Because of the lack of tonal resources of the organ, the lack of ability of the organist, the placement of the piano, the acoustics of the room, or the size of the congregation, it may be necessary to amplify the piano. The top should be raised on a grand piano, and the microphone placed approximately six inches above the middle register strings. With an upright piano, the microphone should be placed approximately twelve inches away from the middle of the soundboard.

Amplified sound should normally be used only during the hymn singing and not at other times, such as during the prelude, offertory, postlude, and so on. If the amplifier and speakers cause the piano to sound distorted in any way with regard to the quality or quantity of sound heard by the congregation, their use should be discontinued.

(b) The need to use pre-taped accompaniments with congregational singing. This involves the use of commercially produced instrumental tracks to accompany the singing of the people. The quality of the amplification system is most important to reproduce as faithfully as possible the signal on the tape. High quality amplifiers and speakers certainly make the difference in this type of experience. False economy in purchasing equipment can greatly limit the use of this technique with congregational experience.

Conclusion

Many physical factors long taken for granted are most significant to the singing of the congregation. Careful consideration of these factors to see if improvements can be made in existing buildings or to insure adequate provision in future buildings in the planning stage can add greatly to the sound of congregational song. In all these areas counsel and advice should be sought from persons qualified and experienced.

The Church Architecture Department of the Sunday School Board will be helpful in consultation in these areas. *The Church Property/Building Guidebook,* compiled by T. Lee Anderton (Convention Press) is a helpful resource both in planning new buildings and in the evaluation of existing buildings.

Chapter 5

PLANNING FOR CONGREGATIONAL SINGING

The singing of a hymn by a group of people is really a simple process. All that is required is that the hymn be familiar and that someone begin the tune. Everything else being ec ial, the group will respond and sing the hymn.

In the dynamic life of a church, the hymn singi of the gregation involves a greater need for planning, careful selection of the hymns, and the preparation for involvement. The planning process is imperative if the experience is to have any relationship to the other parts of the congregational experience. It goes without saying that in planning there are persons to be involved, information to be evaluated, specific hymns to be selected for singing, and decisions to be made as to how and when they will be used. For example, is it effective to sing two hymns consecutively in the same service without any break between them? Does it make any difference whether two hymns closely positioned in the service are in the same key, the same rhythm, or the same mood? Are there psychological reasons for having an upward progression of the keys of hymns leading toward a point of climax in the service, and, likewise, a descending progression of keys of hymns if a decreasing or diminishing emphasis is desired? How may choir rehearsals, department meetings of the religious education organizations, and other program meetings of the church be used to strengthen congregational singing?

The Unity of the Service

Planning for congregational hymn singing follows in sequence the development of church goals and calendar. The corporate experience of hymn singing is not an end in itself, but is a significant part of the corporate life of the congregation—the shared-together experience. While this discussion does not attempt to deal with the planning of the total worship service, it recognizes the fact that a service is most effective when it has unity, logic, and a sense of movement. To the person in the pew, all the pieces of the service should fit together appropriately. When the several components of the service, such as prayer, hymn, announcements, and Scripture reading, do not have a logical progression, it appears as though the order of service was carelessly thrown together at the last minute. To plan a service for the congregation with prayer and careful attention to the available resources and to leave room for God's spirit to work in the hearts of each individual, is to realize the full potential of worship.

The leadership role of the pastor is recognized as he leads in determining the format of the congregational service, usually in presiding over the service, and in his role as preacher, prophet, exhorter. His design for the service and his concern for each part of the service will provide help for the person charged with the selection of the hymns. His guidance in the selection of the closing hymn will be of real value. He may wish to use this hymn as a strong invitation to unbelievers to accept Christ as Savior. Or he may prefer, at times, to use the hymn as a congregational response to the sermon and to extend an invitation to discipleship and church membership. Such planning strengthens the conclusion of the service and brings it to a purposeful climax. To close every service with the singing of "Just As I Am Without One Plea" is to turn a very cherished hymn of commitment into a dull, commonplace experience.

Long-range Planning

The planning process should be approached both in terms of long-range and short-range perspective. Long-range planning should involve the congregational services over a period of twelve to eighteen months. Immediately identifiable guidelines are seasonal emphases—Christmas, Easter, summer, spring, fall, winter, Thanksgiving, and so forth—and those special promotional emphases of significance to the local church, the association, the state convention, and the Southern Baptist Convention.

From the Southern Baptist denominational calendar come some of the month-by-month emphases that will have some influence on the planning of congregational singing if they are to be observed on the church calendar. Several hymns are suggested for each emphasis.

OCTOBER
Outreach Month
Rescue the Perishing, 283
Share His Love, 285
So Send I You, 280
Tell It Out with Gladness, 275
We've a Story to Tell, 281
NOVEMBER
Stewardship and Budget Subscriptions
Because I Have Been Given Much, 414
Give to the Lord, As He Has Blessed You, 415
Glorious Is Thy Name, Most Holy, 419
Lead On, O King Eternal, 420
Something for Thee, 418
We Lift Our Hearts in Songs of Praise, 416
Royal Ambassador Week
We Have a Gospel to Proclaim, 301
Let the Song Go Round the Earth, 306
American Bible Society Day
Christian Men, Arise and Give, 141
Holy Bible, Book Divine, 139
O Word of God Incarnate, 140
Tell It Out with Gladness, 275
Word of God, Across the Ages, 148
DECEMBER
Week of Prayer for Foreign Missions and Lottie Moon Christmas Offering
O Zion, Haste, 295
Send Me, O Lord, Send Me, 293
Send the Light, 304
Tell the Good News, 288
JANUARY
Bible Study Week
Break Thou the Bread of Life, 138

Christian Men, Arise and Give, 141
O Word of God Incarnate, 140
Wonderful Words of Life, 142
Word of God, Across the Ages, 148
Soul Winning Commitment Day
Lord, Lay Some Soul upon My Heart, 298
Lord, Speak to Me, that I May Speak, 276
Make Me a Blessing, 290
Pass It On, 287
People to People, 308
Reach Out and Touch, 314
Send Me, O Lord, Send Me, 293
Set My Soul Afire, 302
Share His Love, 285
So Send I You, 280
Tell the Good News, 288
We Have a Gospel to Proclaim, 301
Baptist Men's Day
God of Grace and God of Glory, 265
Lead On, O King Eternal, 420
Rise Up, O Men of God, 268
Stir Thy Church, O God, Our Father, 269

FEBRUARY

Baptist World Alliance Sunday
All Hail the Power of Jesus' Name, 40,41,42
Let All the World in Every Corner Sing, 24
Let the Song Go Round the Earth, 306
Jesus Shall Reign Where'er the Sun, 282
One World, One Lord, One Witness, 296
Send Me, O Lord, Send Me, 293
Race Relations Sunday
In Christ There is No East or West, 258
Jesus, Friend of Thronging Pilgrims, 100
O Church of God, Triumphant, 237
Reach Out and Touch, 314
Teach Me, O Lord, to Care, 312
Thou, Whose Purpose Is to Kindle, 313
Where Charity and Love Prevail, 257
WMU Focus Week
O Zion, Haste, 295
Send the Light, 304

Tell It Out with Gladness, 275
Tell the Good News, 288
We've a Story to Tell, 281

MARCH

Week of Prayer for Home Missions, and Annie Armstrong Easter Offering
Come, All Christians, Be Committed, 362
Do You Really Care? 316
His Gentle Look, 318
In Christ There Is No East or West, 258
People to People, 308
Reach Out and Touch, 314
Teach Me, O Lord, to Care, 312
To Worship, Work and Witness, 238
When the Church of Jesus, 319

APRIL

Cooperative Program Day
Because I Have Been Given Much, 414
Let the Song Go Round the Earth, 306
One World, One Lord, One Witness, 296
We Lift Our Hearts in Songs of Praise, 416

Doctrinal Emphasis Week
A Charge to Keep I Have, 407
Ask Ye What Great Thing I Know, 60
Lord, Who Dost Give to Thy Church, 239
Teach Me, O Lord, I Pray, 406
Teach Me Thy Way, O Lord, 330
Word of God, Across the Ages, 148

Life Commitment Sunday
A Charge to Keep I Have, 407
God's World Today, 359
He Who Would Valiant Be, 384
Here Is My Life, 356
His Gentle Look, 318
I Have Decided to Follow Jesus, 191
Lord, I Want to Be a Christian, 322
We Are Called to Be God's People, 405
Wherever He Leads I'll Go, 361

MAY

Christian Home Week
God, Give Us Christian Homes, 397

O God in Heaven, Whose Loving Plan, 396
O God, Who to a Loyal Home, 398
Baptist Radio and Television Sunday
Jesus Shall Reign Where'er the Sun, 282
Let All the World in Every Corner Sing, 24
Let the Song Go Round the Earth, 306
O Zion, Haste, 295
One World, One Lord, One Witness, 296

JULY

Christian Citizenship Sunday
A Charge to Keep I Have, 407
O Church of God, Triumphant, 237
My Country, 'Tis of Thee, 511
The Star-Spangled Banner, 512
We Are Called to Be God's People, 405

AUGUST

Church Music Week
All Creatures of Our God and King, 9
I Will Sing of My Redeemer, 465
I Will Sing the Wondrous Story, 53,55
Let All the World in Every Corner Sing, 24
Let the Song Go Round the Earth, 306
My Singing Is a Prayer, 412
O Come, Loud Anthems Let Us Sing, 21
Sing to the Lord of Harvest, 232
Sing We the King, 493
When We All Get to Heaven, 491

SEPTEMBER

Season of Prayer for State Missions
Come, All Christians, Be Committed, 362
People to People, 308
Teach Me, O Lord, to Care, 312
When the Church of Jesus, 319
Sunday School Preparation Week
Christian Men, Arise and Give, 141
Set My Soul Afire, 302
Teach Me, O Lord, I Pray, 406
Tell It Out with Gladness, 275
Wonderful Words of Life, 142
Word of God, Across the Ages, 148

When these emphases are adopted by a church they can become guidelines for long-range planning of congregational services. In order to keep these long-range plans current, they should be updated at least on a quarterly basis.

Short-range Planning

Short-range planning of congregational servies should cover from four to eight weeks. These plans should be quite specific as to objectives, details for each service, individual responsibility and involvement, and the hymns to be shared by the congregation. Short-range plans need to be updated on a weekly basis, maintaining the cutting edge of these specific plans from four to eight weeks ahead. Any negligence at this point can threaten severely the planning process. As each week passes, the forward thrust of the planning period must be advanced another seven days.

Record keeping related to the congregational services is of great help in planning. Those responsible need to determine what kinds of data are needed for reference, for evaluation, and for future planning. Useful data that may be recorded and retained might be:

1. Service music (preludes, offertories, postludes)
2. Choral music
3. Soloists and ensembles
4. Hymns
5. Sermon topics
6. Members of the congregation used in the service to read Scripture, lead in prayer or other acts of worship
7. Scripture Readings read by the congregation

Frequent reference to this information will guard against a too-frequent repetition of service material and too-frequent use of some individuals.

Selection of the Hymns

There may be those rare occasions when the singing itself and the inherent value in that experience may be more important than the hymns involved. The joy of Christian fellowship in singing "psalms, hymns, and spiritual songs" may have value regardless of the songs which are sung. This then takes on the character of a "sing-a-long" and has a valid place in the life of a congregation. It can be a rewarding experience in Christian fellowship. However, to follow this pattern week by week is to fail to recognize the need for awareness of the textual content, and the theological values in the hymns selected. It is wonderful to sing "Blessed assurance, Jesus is mine," and "We're marching to Zion," but we also need to sing "Speak to my heart, Lord Jesus" and "O Master, let me walk with thee." It is exhilarating to sing

>"This is my story, this is my song,
>Praising my Savior, all the day long"

but there is need for the believer to sing with the spirit and the understanding

>"Help me the slow of heart to move
>By some clear, winning word of love;
>Teach me the wayward feet to stay,
>And guide them in the homeward way."

Planning then becomes important because of the need for a careful selection of hymns based on what they say.

When all available information has been gathered for a given congregational service — Sunday morning, Sunday evening, Wednesday evening, or a weeknight evangelistic service—then selections can be made with reason and judgment. That information will include the topic of the sermon, the Scripture to be read, the emphasis of the service, the desired tone and spirit of the service, the number of hymns required, and the position of the hymn within the outline of the service. In addition to that information, the person or persons making hymn selections will draw on a reservoir of knowledge of the hymnal itself and the familiarity of his congregation with its contents. The following concerns should bear on this selection.

The appropriateness of the text is a point of primary concern in this selection. Does it undergird the emphasis, the Scripture, the sermon? Is the hymn an expression of praise addressed to God, such as "Holy, Holy, Holy" (No. 1), or a hymn of praise about God, such as "All Creatures of Our God and King" (No. 9), or a hymn of Christian testimony, such as "My Hope Is Built on Nothing Less" (No. 337), or an invitation to the unbeliever, such as "Let Jesus Come into Your Heart" (No. 179)? Each of these hymns has a distinctive content, extremely useful if properly inserted in the service.

The familiarity of the tune is also of major concern. If the tune is well known, the possibility of hearty participation is very good. If the tune is known by some of the people, the participation will be scattered. If the tune is known by only a few, these few will be singing solos. Surely no music director would select a hymn tune that is totally unknown to everyone in the congregation simply because the text is appropriate. The selection of hymns is done most intelligently by the person who has great familiarity with both the material in the hymnal and the people in the congregation.

The key of the tune and the range of the melody are factors for consideration if the service is an early morning one. Churches that have a regular Sunday morning early service, and also those that have special services, such as a sunrise Easter Sunday service, need to exercise precaution about keys and ranges of the tunes. The accompanists, if able to transpose at sight or from manuscript, can easily solve the problem. But if this solution is not possible, then a hymn tune that lies somewhat high will be difficult for most congregations to sing at an early hour. The increased participation resulting from lowering the keys one or two steps will be quite surprising.

The Contents of the Hymnal

The 1975 edition of *Baptist Hymnal* contains no category indications on the pages as did the previous hymnal. These have been removed to make for greater flexibility in the use of the hymnal. It is possible that many hymns may relate to more than one subject area or classification.

The listing of the contents (page xi) shows the broad sweep of the material in the hymnal. The four basic divisions of the hymnal are: God, God Speaks, God's Work, and God's People. These categories with the subdivisions speak to the many facets of Christian experience and the needs for hymnic literature in the life of the church. The numbers given by each category indicate the hymn numbers in that category.

GOD, 1-137

> **Trinity,** 1-7
> **Father**
>> Praise and Adoration, 8-30
>> Glory and Power, 31-37
> **Jesus Christ**
>> Praise and Adoration, 38-76
>> Advent, 77-79
>> Birth, 80-97

Life and Ministry, 98-104
Suffering and Death, 105-113
Resurrection and Exaltation, 114-126
Return, 127-129
Holy Spirit, 130-137

GOD SPEAKS, 138-149

Bible, 138-142
Christian Heritage, 143-149

GOD'S WORK, 150-234

Creation, 150-155
Redemption
Salvation, 156-163
Grace and Mercy, 164-172
Repentance and Confession, 173-178
Invitation and Acceptance, 179-200
Providence
Guidance and Care, 201-228
Thankfulness, 229-234

GOD'S PEOPLE, 235-506

Church
Foundation and Nature, 235-241
Baptism, 242-244
Lord's Supper, 245-252
Fellowship of Believers, 253-261
Renewal and Revival, 262-273
Evangelism and Missions, 274-307
Social Concern, 308-320
Christian Life
Aspiration, 321-333
Assurance, 334-345
Commitment, 346-373
Faith and Trust, 374-383
Loyalty and Courage, 384-394
Marriage and Family, 395-398
Prayer, 399-404
Service, 405-411
Stewardship, 412-420
Testimony, 421-487
Future Life, 488-506

Special Occasions, 507-512

This content listing speaks to the careful organization of the hymns within the hymnal. The design is a purposeful one so structured to provide songs for congregational singing from a wide variety of subjects. A great diversity exists even within one category. Those responsible for selecting hymns for congregational singing will study carefully these categories and the scope of hymns within each division.

Chapter 6

PREPARATION FOR HYMN SINGING

The Music Director's Responsibility

When the hymns have been selected for the service, the music director will examine the hymns—both texts and tunes—to anticipate any difficulty that might occur in the congregation's singing. Normally all stanzas will be used. If for some reason stanzas must be omitted, the omissions must be noted and communicated. If the ushers are accustomed to waiting for the fourth stanza to come down the aisle to take the offering, and only three stanzas are to be sung, they should know that.

If a final "amen" is to be used on a hymn, that fact should be noted and communicated to the accompanists. Sometimes an "amen" may be added to a hymn where none is included in the hymnal. This is entirely appropriate and can be done without any difficulty if both the accompanists and the choir know it is being done.

The traditional use of *fermatas* in familiar hymn tunes is a practice that varies from one congregation to another. In the copy editing of *Baptist Hymnal,* 1975 it was decided to remove most of the fermatas and other markings on the music. This gives greater flexibility for the congregation and the leader. Some hymns which congregations generally sing observing a fermata which does not occur in the music, and some which have fermatas written in the music, are listed below. The director will determine how they will be treated and be in agreement with the accompanists regarding that treatment.

9.   "All Creatures of Our God and King"
     The fermata written in the second line at the end of the second "Alleluia" is usually observed.

37. "A Mighty Fortress Is Our God"
     The fermatas in the second and third lines are best treated as dotted half notes and kept in tempo.

41. "All Hail the Power of Jesus' Name" (DIADEM)
     Sometimes a fermata is observed in the second line, fourth measure, on the word "fall." If a congregation is singing unaccompanied and undirected, they seem to want to pause at this cadence. It doesn't seem to do any violence to the sturdiness of the tune as long as the tempo is resumed on "Bring forth the royal diadem."

130. "Pentecostal Power"
     Usually a fermata is observed on the word "Lord" at the beginning of the refrain and again in the middle of the fourth line. The original tempo is resumed in the following measure each time.

205. "There Is a Balm in Gilead"
     The traditional fermata in the final cadence of the stanza (the end of the fourth line) has been replaced by notation that gives the same effect while keeping the tempo steady.

210. "Come, Come, Ye Saints"
     Usually a fermata is observed in the third line, second measure, second beat, on the word "day." This may also be treated as a half note and kept in tempo. The changes of meters from 4/4 to 3/4 in this tune should cause no difficulty as long as the quarter note beat is maintained steadily.

216. "Great Is Thy Faithfulness"
     Usually a slight slowing occurs in the final phrase of the refrain (the last four measures), and a fermata is observed at the syllable "ness," leading to a slower pace on the words, "Lord, unto me."

274. "Christ Is the World's True Light"
     There is no time signature in this tune because in the cadences at the ends of lines one and two, fermatas have been replaced by dotted half notes and they are

kept in tempo. Otherwise the tune is in 4/4.

293. "Send Me, O Lord, Send Me"
Usually a fermata is observed in the fourth line, second measure, on the word "be." It seems to occur naturally at this peak of the ascending melodic line before the final phrase.

299. "New Life for You"
Usually a fermata is observed in the fourth line, second measure, on the word "King." This is the peak of the ascending melodic line and the fermata seems to give greater strength to the final phrase.

348. "Living for Jesus"
Usually a fermata is observed in the final line of the refrain on the word "live."

352. "I Am Thine, O Lord"
Usually a fermata is observed in the final line of the refrain on the word "Lord."

360. "Beneath the Cross of Jesus"
Frequently a fermata is observed in the fourth line, second measure, third beat, on the word "heat." Unaccompanied and undirected congregations seem to do this naturally.

383. "How Firm a Foundation"
In the second line, the fourth measure, the final note is sometimes sung as notated, and at other times it is held as though observing a fermata. Sometimes when this is done, the half note on the word "Word" is treated as a whole note tied to a half note and the cadence kept in tempo, which adds two full beats in 2/2.

424. "Jesus Is All the World to Me"
Sometimes a fermata is observed in the fourth line, third measure, on the word "glad."

432. "Wonderful, Wonderful Jesus"
Sometimes a fermata is observed in the final line of the refrain on the word "strength."

487. "Since Jesus Came into My Heart"
At the beginning of the refrain, the word "since" is observed as having a fermata, as is the word "roll" in the final line.

In addition to observing fermatas that are not there, congregations have also developed some generally accepted ways of taking liberties with tempos by elongating phrases, or stretching measures, thereby exercising some rhythmic freedom. We refer to a momentary fluctuation of speed or tempo as *rubato*. *Rubato* is an Italian word that literally means "robbed." Some hymn tunes which are usually sung in this way are listed below.

109. "Blessed Redeemer"
      The last two lines of the refrain are usually sung with a good deal of freedom, which seems to cause no difficulty to the congregation.

121. "Look, Ye Saints! The Sight Is Glorious"
      A slackening of pace usually occurs in the fourth line, first measure, because the basic quarter note and half note pattern of the first three lines gives way to a pattern of eighth notes and quarter notes. This one measure distinctly requires a bit slower tempo to sing with ease.

127. "One Day"
      The last two measures of the refrain are usually sung at a slower pace for dramatic emphasis.

129. "What If It Were Today?"
      Sometimes the fourth line of the stanza, measures one and two are sung with a sudden slowness, a slight fermata on the word "wide," followed by a return to tempo in measures three and four. There is also a broadening in the last two measures of the refrain.

438. "He Lives"
      In the final line of the refrain, the last four measures are usually sung with greater freedom, with some slight hold on the word "lives" both times it occurs.

493. "Sing We the King" (and 497, "O That Will Be Glory")
      Since the texts of both hymns are set to the same tune, the comments will apply to both. A gradual slowing of the pace usually occurs in the last four measures of the stanza with the refrain beginning in tempo. Considerable freedom is exercised in the last four measures of the refrain with a fermata usually observed in the third measure from the end, the second beat, as the melody leaps the octave and holds momentarily.

Some of the newer hymns in *Baptist Hymnal,* 1975 reflect a contemporary influence in rhythmic structure within the measure or some rhythmic structures not in previous hymnals. All these should be examined carefully by the music director before they are shared with the congregation. Any uncertainty on the part of the director or the accompanists in handling such rhythmic structures will be confusing to the congregation.

These contemporary patterns are heard every day. They just have not been in our hymnal before. It will be helpful to point out some of these specific tunes and supply a word of explanation.

14. "Praise the Lord"
   The divided beats, for example, in measures one and three can be sung easily if the tempo is not too hurried. Take it slowly and it all falls into line very nicely.

18. "Praise Him, O Praise Him" (See example 13)
   Divided beats appear frequently. Note that the tune is really contained in the first four measures. It is in the key of F, back to D for the final statement.

21. "O Come, Loud Anthems" (See example 14)
   This is a rhythmic German chorale melody of the seventeenth century. Sing it rhythmically with three steady beats per measure.

49. "For the Beauty of the Earth" (RAYMER)
   The divided fourth beats in the first line on the words "raise" and "praise" sing easily and without any stress or accent. They simply slip in half a beat before the downbeat of the following measure.

77. "Comfort, Comfort Ye My People" (See example 15)
   This sixteenth-century French psalm tune is similar to the tune discussed above, No. 21. The final measures in the first and second lines contain four beats; otherwise a steady three beats per measure make the tune move along vigorously.

186. "Just As I Am" (TABERNACLE) (See example 16)
   This new tune for a well-known text goes very well. The ends of the phrases need to be held carefully and released properly. The longest of these is on the word "God," which extends for seven beats. Teach the choir to sing this correctly and you will help the congregation bring the tune off with real meaning.

225. Have No Fear, Little Flock" (See example 17)
   The sixteenth note on the second beat of measures

one, two, and five, should be sung gently, not quickly
or with undue accent.

228.   "Surely Goodness and Mercy"
        The dotted eighth and sixteenth notes in the refrain, a
        melodic pattern that does not occur in the stanza,
        seems to indicate a slower tempo than the stanza sug-
        gests. The triplet figure on the second page, second
        and third lines, occurs on the third beat. Be sure it is
        not as three eighth notes beginning on the last half of
        the second beat of the measure.

239.   "Lord, Who Dost Give to Thy Church" (See example
        18)
        The first and fourth lines begin on the second beat of
        the measure, with the accompaniment beginning on
        the first beat. Confidence on the part of the choir will
        give assurance to the congregation. (The same second-
        beat entrance occurs in the tune SINE NOMINE, 43, 144).

306.   "Let the Song Go Round the Earth"
        The triplet figures occurring in measures 1, 5, 10, 12,
        and 14, should be treated as though the measures
        were in 12/8 instead of 4/4. Keep the triplet figures
        even and the tune will sing quite easily.

308.   "People to People"
        The tied eighth notes, usually tying the last half of the
        second beat to the first half of the third beat, occur fre-
        quently throughout the tune and are intended to
        emphasize the word that is sung at that point. The
        notational values of the phrase are designed to match
        the spoken inflections of the text.

331.   "Free to Be Me" (See example 19)
        With no time signature, keep the quarter note the basic
        beat note throughout. Note tempo suggestion in appen-
        dix.

384.   "He Who Would Valiant Be" (See example 20)
        With no time signature, it is suggested that the quarter
        note be maintained as the basic beat note throughout.
        The first two lines may be basically 3/4. The third line
        has two measures of 6/4, and the fourth line ends with
        three measures of 4/4. Don't worry about the patterns;
        just keep the quarter note beat going.

There are other decisions that the music director will want to make regarding some of the following possibilities:

1. If both organ and piano are used in the service, consider the use of only one or the other on some of the stanzas of a hymn. This will awaken new interest and offer variety in the using of the hymn. It may be planned like this:

Introduction: Organ
Stanza 1—Organ and Piano
Stanza 2—Organ
Stanza 3—Piano
Stanza 4—Organ and Piano

2. The congregation may sing a stanza of a hymn without accompaniment and without any word of explanation. Of course, you must prepare the organist and pianist who need to know exactly when to play. Inform the choir also, so they will know what to expect. The unaccompanied singing adds another refreshing dimension to the hymn.

Introduction: Organ
Stanza 1—Organ and Piano
Stanza 2—Organ
Stanza 3—Unaccompanied
Stanza 4—Organ and Piano

The use of the unaccompanied stanza can vary with the hymn. If the mood and text of the hymn are quiet with some restraint, the final stanza may be unaccompanied. Examples are "Jesus, Keep Me Near the Cross," "Speak to My Heart, Lord Jesus," "Near to the Heart of God," or "Sweet, Sweet Spirit."

3. An interlude by the organ or piano before a final stanza can be most effective, depending on the skill of the instrumentalist. This interlude may be improvisatory, or may simply involve the use of the final phrase of the tune. For example, after the third stanza of "Take the Name of Jesus with You," (No. 473), the organist may continue in tempo with the fourth-beat pickup into the last four measures of the refrain. The congregation may then sing the fourth stanza. This needs to be rehearsed carefully with the organist, pianist, and choir. With everyone involved understanding the plan, no difficulty should arise and the attention of the congregation will be held by this unannounced and unexplained venture.

Introduction: Organ
Stanza 1—Organ and Piano
Stanza 2—Organ

18 Praise Him, O Praise Him

1. Praise him, O praise him, Praise the
   Lord for all his blessings; Praise him, O
   praise him, Sing a joyful song before him;
   Praise him, O praise him, Sing a
   joyful, jubilant song.

2. Glory and honor, Glory
   be to God the Father; Glory and
   honor To the Son and Holy Spirit;

*A-MEN.

* The spoken "Amen" is an optional ending for the second stanza.
Words, Mary Lou Reynolds, 1970. Tune PASCHALL, William J. Reynolds, 1970. © Copyright 1970
Broadman Press. All rights reserved.

Example 13

O Come, Loud Anthems Let Us Sing 21

1. O come, loud anthems let us sing, Loud thanks to our Almighty King; For we our voices high should raise, When our salvation's Rock we praise.
2. Into his presence let us haste, To thank him for his favors past; To him address, in joyful songs, The praise that to his name belongs.
3. The depths of earth are in his hand, Her secret wealth at his command; The strength of hills that reach the skies, Subjected to his empire lies.
4. O let us to his courts repair, And bow with adoration there; Down on our knees, devoutly all, Before the Lord, our Maker, fall.

Psalm 95:1-6. Words, Tate and Brady's *New Version,* 1696. Tune HERR JESU CHRIST, *Cantionale Germanicum,* Dresden, 1628.

Example 14

77 Comfort, Comfort Ye My People

1. Com-fort, com-fort ye my peo-ple, Speak ye peace, thus saith our God;
2. Hark, the voice of one that cri-eth In the des-ert far and near,
3. Make ye straight what long was crook-ed, Make the rough-er plac-es plain;

Com-fort those who sit in dark-ness, Mourn-ing 'neath their sor-rows' load.
Bid-ding all men to re-pent-ance Since the king-dom now is here.
Let your hearts be true and hum-ble, As be-fits his ho-ly reign.

Speak ye to Je-ru-sa-lem Of the peace that waits for them;
O that warn-ing cry o-bey! Now pre-pare for God a way;
For the glo-ry of the Lord Now o'er earth is shed a-broad;

Tell her that her sins I cov-er, And her war-fare now is o-ver.
Let the val-leys rise to meet him, And the hills bow down to greet him.
And all flesh shall see the to-ken That his word is nev-er bro-ken. A-MEN.

Isaiah 40:1-8. Words, Johannes Olearius, 1671; translated, Catherine Winkworth, 1863. Tune
PSALM 42, *Genevan Psalter*, 1551.

Example 15

186 Just As I Am

1. Just as I am, with-out one plea, But that thy
2. Just as I am, and wait-ing not To rid my
3. Just as I am, thy love un-known Has bro-ken

blood was shed for me, And that thou
soul of one dark blot, To thee whose
ev-'ry bar-rier down; Now to be

bidd'st me come to thee,
blood can cleanse each spot, O Lamb of God,
thine, yea, thine a-lone,

(after last stanza)

I come. I come.

Words, Charlotte Elliott, 1834. Tune TABERNACLE, Phillip Landgrave, 1968. © Copyright 1968 Broadman Press. All rights reserved.

Example 16

Have No Fear, Little Flock 225

Unison

1. Have no fear, lit-tle flock, have no fear, lit-tle
2. Have good cheer, lit-tle flock, have good cheer, lit-tle
3. Praise the Lord high a-bove, praise the Lord high a-
4. Thank-ful hearts raise to God, thank-ful hearts raise to

flock, for the Fa-ther has cho-sen to
flock, for the Fa-ther will keep you in
bove, for he stoops down to heal you, up-
God, for he stays close be-side you, in

give you the King-dom, Have no fear, lit-tle flock!
his love for-ev-er, Have good cheer, lit-tle flock!
lift and re-store you, Praise the Lord high a-bove!
all things works with you, Thank-ful hearts raise to God!

Words, st. 1, Luke 12:32; st. 2-4, Marjorie Jillson, 1972. Tune LITTLE FLOCK 1971,
Heinz Werner Zimmermann, 1971. From *Five Hymns* by Heinz Werner Zimmermann, copyright 1973
by Concordia Publishing House. Used by permission.

Example 17

239   Lord, Who Dost Give to Thy Church

Unison

1. Lord, who dost give to thy church for its heal-ing
2. Clear be the voic-es of preach-ers and proph-ets
3. Ten-der and wise be the hearts of the pas-tors,
4. May those who teach grow in knowl-edge and pa-tience,
5. Lord, ev-er give to us gifts in due mea-sure,

Gifts, and the grace to sus-tain and re-new,
Fear-less-ly speak-ing the word of the Lord,
Guid-ing and guard-ing the souls in their care,
Guid-ing to wis-dom the young and the old,
Each need-ing oth-er, and all hav-ing worth;

Hear as we pray that to-day and each mor-row
Word of re-demp-tion thro' God's Son in-car-nate,
Firm with the way-ward, a strength to the doubt-ing,
Train-ing for wor-ship and wit-ness and ser-vice,
So to the Fa-ther, the Son, and the Spir-it,

We to thy pur-pose may show our-selves true.
Bless-ing for curs-ing, and peace for the sword.
Help-ing the need-y their bur-dens to bear.
Foes to all false-hood, in truth-ful-ness bold.
Glo-ry be shown by the church here on earth. A-MEN.

Example 18

331 Free to Be Me

1. Free to be me, God, I real-ly am free; Free to be
2. Free-dom, pos-ses-sion that makes me like you, Fright-ens me,
3. Free to live ful-ly, to fol-low your way, Give my-self

come what you want me to be; Free to de-cide wheth-er
God, when its mean-ing seeps through; Bless-ing or curse, Lord, con-
whol-ly, to die ev-'ry day; Free to be real, God, to

I should be lord, Or be your slave and o-bey your word.
demned to be free? Free, but re-spon-si-ble, free to be me.
strip off my mask, Be your cre-a-tion, it's all that I ask.

Words, Kate Wilkins Woolley, 1970. Tune CHISLEHURST, William L. Hooper, 1970. © Copyright 1970
Broadman Press. All rights reserved.

Example 19

He Who Would Valiant Be 384

1. He who would val - iant be 'Gainst all di - sas - ter,
2. Who so be - set him round With dis - mal sto - ries;
3. Since, Lord, thou dost de - fend Us with thy Spir - it,

Let him in con - stan - cy Fol - low the Mas - ter.
Do but them - selves con - found; His strength the more is.
We know we at the end Shall life in - her - it.

There's no dis - cour - age - ment Shall make him once re - lent
No foes shall stay his might, Tho he with gi - ants fight;
Then, fan - cies, flee a - way! I'll fear not what men say;

His first a - vowed in - tent To be a pil - grim.
He will make good his right To be a pil - grim.
I'll la - bor night and day To be a pil - grim. A - MEN.

Words, John Bunyan, 1684; adapted, Percy Dearmer, 1906. Words from *The English Hymnal.* Used by permission of Oxford University Press. Tune ST. DUNSTAN'S, C. Winfred Douglas, 1917. Music used by permission of The Church Pension Fund.

Example 20

Stanza 3—Piano
Interlude—Organ repeats last phrase of tune in tempo
Stanza 4—Organ and Piano

If the interlude is improvisatory, there must be some under-standing as to the number of measures involved (probably four) and how the cadence will end. Sometimes the interlude can end on the dominant and the final stanza will then begin in tempo. Again, the music director, the organist, the pianist, and the choir all need to know how this is to occur and must be prepared to be an intelligent part of the experience.

4. Free accompaniments are discussed in Chapter 3, and do not need further explanation here, except that the decision to use or not to use one must be made by the music director in the light of the knowledge of the hymn tune itself, the free accompaniment repertoire of the organist, and the responsiveness of the con-gregation to this technique. The plan to use a free accompaniment might be the one outlined below.

Introduction: Organ
Stanza 1—Organ and Piano
Stanza 2—Piano
Stanza 3—Unaccompanied
Stanza 4—Organ plays free accompaniment and piano plays
          hymn tune melody in octaves or double octaves

5. Instruments other than the organ and piano may be used. These are discussed in Chapter 3, and can add genuine interest to the hymn singing. Consider the following plan.

Introduction: Piano
Stanza 1—Organ and Piano
Stanza 2—Handbells
Stanza 3—Unaccompanied
Stanza 4—Organ, Piano, and Handbells

Rehearsing the Hymns with the Organist and Pianist

Outside of the close relationship between the music director and the pastor, there is no greater need for clear understanding and communication than exists between the music director and the organist and pianist. As far as the hymn singing of the con-gregation is concerned, the latter relationship is most important. The music director is responsible for the hymn singing, the spirit of the singing, the involvement of the people, and the supporting role of the choir. The organist and pianist are responsible for playing the instruments as skillfully as possible to contribute in the most effective manner.

All of this happens with greater effectiveness if the leader and accompanists have a regular weekly discussion leading to an understanding of the tunes to be sung during the following Sunday services. The problems inherent in each tune can be discussed freely. While there may not be unanimous agreement concerning tempo or dynamics, there can be a clear understanding as to how the music director intends to direct it in the Sunday service. Playing through every tune to be sung by the congregation may seem unnecessary and foolish, particularly if the tunes are old familiar favorites. But even where well-known hymns are involved a meeting of the minds can improve the congregational response and heighten the joy of hymn singing for everyone. The following should be discussed and rehearsed together.

1. The introduction of the tune must be agreed upon. How much of the tune shall be played, and at what level of volume? What registration will be used, and how does it relate to that used at the beginning of the first stanza when the congregation sings? The introduction sets the tempo and the mood and gives the key of the tune. If those factors are clear to the congregation, the hymn singing will go much better.

2. The tempo of the tune needs to be clearly understood and accepted. If there is a difference of opinion in the service regarding the tempo—if the music director wishes the tune sung faster or slower and the instruments do not follow the director, the congregation will continue to follow the instruments. The risk of that happening is much less if an attempt is made to come to agreement prior to the service.

3. The style of the accompaniment—whether it should be legato or slightly staccato—can be determined for each hymn tune. Also, the matter of the release of the sound of the organ at the ends of the phrases needs to be discussed.

4. The registration of the organ should be discussed. The sound of different ranks of pipes and combinations of ranks can be evaluated with regard to the hymn singing. A record of the registration used on each stanza of each hymn can be helpful in an evaluation session following the service.

5. Some agreement needs to be reached about the volume of sound from the instruments. The music director will be in the best position to suggest the use of either more or less sound for

the hymn singing. There should be enough volume with the proper registration to fully support hearty singing from the congregation. Too little sound from the instruments provides no encouragement for the people to sing out. Too much sound overpowers them and discourages singing.

Taping the Hymn Singing

One of the most helpful ways to evaluate the singing of the congregation in a service is to record the sound on some type of recording equipment. This can be done easily with a cassette recorder, and the center balcony seems to afford an excellent place for the microphone. The tape will capture the total sound of the hymn singing—the congregation, the choir, and the accompanying instruments.

Careful listening to this tape after the service will give helpful clues as to the balance of sound, the registrations, the togetherness of instruments and congregation, the introductions and the tempos. An evaluation procedure of this sort continuing for several weeks can prove most informative and helpful. Significant improvement in congregational hymn singing will occur without the congregation's being aware of the process.

If the music director and accompanists have a commitment to improve the hymn singing, a willingness to work together completely, and a cooperative spirit toward the problem, the singing of the congregation can show noticeable improvement.

Chapter 7

BROADENING CONGREGATIONAL REPERTOIRE OF HYMNS

How many hymns in the hymnal does your congregation know well and welcome the opportunity to sing? Congregations read the English language much better than they read music notation. Unfamiliarity with the hymn tune is the basic barrier to a person's participation in congregational singing. A director's failure to recognize this fact and his failure to teach unfamiliar tunes until they are familiar result in less and less participation.

The number of hymns that the congregation knows and will readily sing varies from church to church. Familiar hymns are used frequently for two basic reasons: (1) the congregation likes to sing them, and (2), if we use them almost everyone will sing. This is logical reasoning and it works. Such practice is not to be faulted unless the music leader fails to increase the number of familiar hymns and thereby to widen the circle of resources for congregational singing.

To sing regularly from the same handful of hymns leads to stagnation, and this practice continued over a long period will result in a decreasing number of hymns the congregation knows. New hymns and tunes need to be brought to the knowledge of the congregation for they add to spiritual maturity and growth.

A Musical Problem

Helping the congregation learn a new song is largely a musical problem. The text can be read with no difficulty, but the ready reading of the musical notation is another problem. The careful teaching of the tune involves patience, repetition, and constant reassurance. It also involves strategic planning for using all available resources in order to get maximum participation.

First, the music director must know the song. He must fully comprehend it musically and textually. He cannot teach something he himself does not possess in his mind. The confidence which he reflects and his love of the song will be apparent. At this point of teaching he will not use any background material about the text, tune, author, or composer. He needs to be able to sing the tune with confidence and to encourage the singing of the tune on the part of others.

Second, the music leader needs to take advantage of any opportunity to share the new song. Anywhere he can confront a segment of his congregation is an opportunity to say "let me share with you this new song." Department meetings of the church's educational program as well as meetings of the Woman's Missionary Union or the Brotherhood, parents' meetings, deacons' meetings, and so on, offer great opportunities to share the excitement of a new song. All these groups together make up a major portion of the church's congregation.

Third, the music leader will involve all those persons who have responsibility for leading the singing in any organizational component of the church. Those include the music leaders and instrumentalists of the Sunday School and Training Union departments, who, each week, lead a segment of the congregation. The music leader can teach these individuals the new song and inspire them to become familiar with it and share it enthusiastically with the groups they lead.

Methods of Teaching

The teaching of new hymns to the congregation should be done carefully and with design. The number of new hymns that a congregation will accept and use will vary from church to church. Some congregations will readily accept a new hymn each month, while others will do well to learn one every two or three months. The music director must determine the frequency with which he can use new material. If he is wise in his decision, the hymn singing will be strengthened. If he chooses to move faster than his congregation desires, he will encounter passive resistance, and the response of the congregation to his leadership in teaching new hymns will be weakened.

Suggestions for introducing new hymns to the congregation:

1. Use opportunities with strong motivational factors, such as revivals or witness experiences, retreats or camps, and congregational services in which a new hymn may support a sermon topic, a seasonal emphasis, a churchwide theme or emphasis, or the ordinances.

In these experiences, the fact that a new hymn relates to a theme, has a specific reason for being presented, or has unusual meaning offers valid reasons for bringing it to the attention of the congregation. New songs that have been used as theme songs for evangelistic efforts have become very familiar and remain in the repertoire of congregational songs long after the event for which they were first used has passed.

2. Tell the congregation about the new hymn. The church bulletin or weekly paper can be used to explain that you are going to lead a new hymn in the service the following Sunday. Also, the congregation can be told that the hymn will be sung in each Sunday School department as a rehearsal for the church service.

The interest and enthusiasm of the music leader should be reflected in these printed communications. Sometimes brief, terse statements about the author or composer may be helpful, but this information needs to be used to capture interest without becoming tiresome with boring details. "Amazing Grace! How Sweet the Sound" has been sung effectively for almost two centuries by people who did not know of the colorful life of John Newton, a clergyman in the Church of England who wrote the hymn. Such information as this will bring greater interest and enrichment after the hymn is known, but it will not help someone overcome the initial barrier of learning the tune and of being able to sing it.

3. Some definite plan of adding to the congregation's hymn repertoire is desired. A hymn-of-the-month plan, or a select list (four or six or more) of "New Hymns for Our Church This Year" will give some direction.

The suggested Hymn-of-the-Month plan promoted by the Church Music Department of the Sunday School Board and carried in the music periodicals is being reinstituted after being discontinued for several years. This plan is recommended and resources are provided to help those churches who wish to follow this plan. It is suggested that the music director discuss the hymns with the pastor and the church leadership and begin the Hymn-of-the-Month plan with the unanimous support of the church leaders.

Some churches may prefer to select their own hymns. In these instances, it may be advisable to involve a number of people in the selection of the hymns. The pastor and the music director, or a special committee may select the unfamiliar hymns to be learned. The adult choir or the adult and youth choirs together might share in the decision making. Such involvement tends to generate greater interest and heighten participation.

4. Using unfamiliar tunes as service music by the organ and/or piano may be helpful to the members of the congregation if they know what is being played. Unless they have reason to know that their attention needs to be focused on the tune they will hear, there will be little chance of any learning being accomplished. Without this knowledge the congregation will passively accept this music as more unfamiliar, unidentifiable organ or piano music. People do not learn new tunes by accident in some strange process of osmosis.

This is true also of the use of a choral arrangement of the hymn-of-the-month sung by the choir.

The most effective use of the choir occurs at the time the congregation sings the hymn. The choir members should have learned the tune prior to this service. Their hearty singing reinforcing the congregation can be most helpful.

5. New texts which are unfamiliar to the congregation may be sung to familiar tunes that the congregation already knows. In this way a specific text, appropriate for a particular occasion or sermon subject, may be used in the church service effectively without having to teach a new tune to the congregation. There are a number of hymns in *Baptist Hymnal,* 1975 that have alternate tunes given at the bottom of the page. Some of these are:

    8   Praise, My Soul, the King of Heaven
        (alternate tune REGENT SQUARE, No. 87)
  121   Look, Ye Saints! The Sight Is Glorious
        (alternate tune REGENT SQUARE, No. 87)
  221   Sometimes a Light Surprises
        (alternate tune AURELIA, No. 236)
  286   I Bless the Christ of God
        (alternate tune ST. THOMAS, 240)

292 Ye Servants of God
     (alternate tune LYONS, No. 30)
362 Come, All Christians, Be Committed
     (alternate tune HYFRYDOL, No. 11)
439 God Moves in a Mysterious Way
     (alternate tune ST. ANNE, No. 223)
450 I'm Not Ashamed to Own My Lord
     (alternate tune SERENITY, No. 329)
464 How Sweet the Name of Jesus Sounds
     (alternate tune ORTONVILLE, No. 267, repeat
     final line of each stanza)
470 O Thou to Whose All-Searching Sight
     (alternate tunes OLD 100TH, No. 6; and
     DUKE STREET, No. 282)

Other possible matching of unfamiliar texts to familiar tunes are:

20   God of Earth and Outer Space
     (alternate tune MARTYN, 172)
21   O Come, Loud Anthems Let Us Sing
     (alternate tune OLD 100TH, No. 17)
100 Jesus, Friend of Thronging Pilgrims
     (alternate tune REGENT SQUARE, No. 87)
224 Give to the Winds Your Fears
     (alternate tune DIADEMATA, No. 52)
238 To Worship, Work, and Witness
     (alternate tunes AURELIA, No. 236; and LANCASHIRE, No.
     237)
247 From Every Race, from Every Clime
     (alternate tunes ARLINGTON, No. 68; and MCKEE, No. 258)
269 Stir Thy Church, O God, Our Father
     (alternate tunes BEECHER, No. 3; HYFRYDOL, No. 11; and
     HYMN TO JOY, No. 31)
274 Christ Is the World's True Light
     (alternate tune NUN DANKET, No. 234)
313 Thou, Whose Purpose Is to Kindle
     (alternate tune STUTTGART, No. 36)
385 Once to Every Man and Nation
     (alternate tunes BEECHER, No. 3; HYFRYDOL, No. 11; and
     HYMN TO JOY, No. 31)
398 O God, Who to a Loyal Home
     (alternate tune KINGSFOLD, 57)
400 Prayer Is the Soul's Sincere Desire

(alternate tunes ARLINGTON, No. 68; ORTONVILLE, No. 267; and ST. AGNES, No. 133)

402   I Waited for the Lord
      (alternate tunes AVON, No. 113; MCKEE, No. 258; and OR-
      TONVILLE, No. 267)

445   God Loved the World So That He Gave
      (alternate tunes CANONBURY, No. 276; GERMANY, No. 301)

456   So Let Our Lips and Lives Express
      (alternate tunes CANONBURY, No. 276; GERMANY, No. 301;
      and ST. AGNES, No. 133)

460   Fill Thou My Life, O Lord My God
      (alternate tunes ARLINGTON, No. 68; ST. AGNES, No. 133;
      and ORTONVILLE, No. 267)

476   The Savior's Wondrous Love
      (alternate tune ST. THOMAS, No. 268)

504   There Is a Land of Pure Delight
      (alternate tune ST. PETER, No. 249)

6. Rehearsals of hymn singing by the congregation can be effective and interesting. Mid-week or Sunday evening services seem to offer a more relaxed and informal atmosphere for such experience. It is possible to rehearse a single hymn on Sunday morning a few minutes before the beginning of the service.

The music director and the accompanists should plan carefully these rehearsals with the congregation. The leading and the playing should be well coordinated as to make the experience enjoyable and comfortable for the congregation. The tempo, the mood, and the level of instrumental sound are items of concern to be worked out in advance. A harmonious meeting of minds will help the teaching of the congregation go much easier. If the accompaniment for the singing is too fast, or too slow, or too loud, or too soft, the leader will be frustrated and the congregation confused.

The teaching procedure may involve the accompanying instrument giving out the melody line without any harmonization, after which the people sing the melody in unison. In this manner the sound of the harmonic structure does not clutter the learning process at the outset. In like manner, the leader may "line out" the tune, by singing a line at a time with the congregation repeating the line he sings. Repeating the first stanza two or three times helps to etch the tune in the learner's mind and to focus attention on the tune rather than the words. After the tune is in hand, other stanzas may be used.

7. The choir can help in the teaching and in the singing of a new or unfamiliar hymn by singing a stanza which is repeated by the congregation. The music director will need to decide whether the choir will sing most effectively in parts or in unison.

In the choir rehearsal prior to the service when a new hymn will be used, the choir should become very familiar with the hymn. Attention may be called to the musical characteristics of the tune, the content, the text, and other related facts to heighten the significance of the hymn to the choir.

It is helpful to point out to the choir members that during the congregational hymn singing in the service, the choir actually is a part of the congregation. The idea of sharing in the hymn singing as part of the congregation is much more helpful than the concept of being isolated performers singing the hymn *to* the congregation.

Chapter 8

THE METRICAL FORMS OF HYMNS

Some understanding of the metrical forms of hymns will be helpful to one who is responsible for leading congregational singing. Since hymns are poetic expressions, it is not unusual that we find terminology related to poetry used in connection with hymn texts. The iambic foot, the trochaic foot, the dactylic foot, the anapestic foot, are found in all hymnic literature. Stanza form and rhyme scheme are evident to one who looks carefully at the text. Because the hymn texts are placed between the staves of music, the poetic structure of the text may not be readily apparent.

A system of symbols and terminology peculiar to the area of hymn study has developed across many years. Hymnic meters attempt to classify texts (and the tunes to which they are sung) into categories on the basis of the number of lines per stanza and the number of syllables per line. Except for the three most frequently found meters—common, long, and short—they will be indicated by a series of digits: 8.7.8.7.; 10.10.10.10.; 14.14.4.7.8. and so on. The number of digits shown indicates the number of lines per stanza, and each digit indicates the number of syllables in that line.

For example, the meter for "How Firm a Foundation" (No. 383) is 11.11.11.11. This means that each stanza has four lines, and each line has eleven syllables. The metrical form, 8.7.8.7., indicates that each stanza has four lines, and the first and third

lines have eight syllables each; the second and fourth lines have
seven syllables each. This is the meter for "Jesus Calls Us." The
addition of *D* to these numbers as in 8.7.8.7.D. (for "Come, Thou
Fount of Every Blessing," No. 13), indicates that each stanza has
eight lines, or a four-line stanza doubled. This might also be written 8.7.8.7.8.7.8.7.

In the *Baptist Hymnal,* 1975, the hymn meters are given in the
Alphabetical Index of Tunes. (pp. 550-554) The hymn tune name
is given at the bottom of the page below each hymn. This name,
then, is located in the Alphabetical Listing of tunes and the metrical form of the tune is indicated. If one wishes to find other tunes
of a like meter, the Metrical Index of Tunes (pp. 554-557) will
provide that information.

The three metrical forms most commonly found are usually indicated by initials rather than by digits: C.M. (common meter);
L.M. (long meter); and S.M. (short meter).

Common meter (C.M.) is a four-line stanza in 8.6.8.6. meter.
This is the Old English ballad meter, originally two poetic lines
containing seven iambic feet, or fourteen syllables. This couplet,
known as a "fourteener," breaks into four lines of alternating
four and three feet, or eight and six syllables. Some familiar common meter hymns are:

"Amazing Grace! How Sweet the Sound" (No. 165)
"Am I a Soldier of the Cross" (No. 388)
"All Hail the Power of Jesus' Name" (No. 40)
The rhyme is abab:

"O God, our help in ages past,	(8 syllables) a
Our hope for years to come,	(6 syllables) b
Our shelter from the stormy blast,	(8 syllables) a
And our eternal home!"	(6 syllables) b

(No. 223)

or *abcb*

"In Christ there is no East or West,	(8 syllables) a
In him no South or North;	(6 syllables) b
But one great fellowship of love	(8 syllables) c
Thro'out the whole wide earth."	(6 syllables) b

(No. 258)

Long meter (L.M.) is a four-line stanza, each line containing
eight syllables, 8.8.8.8. The form follows the iambic-dimeter pattern of the early Latin hymns. Some of the familiar long meter
hymns are:

"Praise God from Whom All Blessings Flow" (No. 6)
"Just As I Am" (No. 187)
"Jesus Shall Reign Where'er the Sun" (No. 282)
The rhyme is:

"When I survey the wondrous cross	(8 syllables) a
On which the Prince of Glory died	(8 syllables) b
My richest gain I count but loss,	(8 syllables) a
And pour contempt on all my pride."	(8 syllables) b

(No. 111)

or *aabb*:

"Children of the heavenly Father	(8 syllables) a
Safely in his bosom gather;	(8 syllables) a
Nestling bird nor star in heaven	(8 syllables) b
Such a refuge e'er was given."	(8 syllables) b

(No. 209)

Short meter (S.M.) is a four-line stanza in 6.6.8.6. meter. This poetic meter was once called "Poulter's Measure," because of the poulterers' custom of giving twelve eggs for the first dozen and thirteen or fourteen for the second. The couplet of twelve and fourteen syllables breaks into a four-line stanza. Some familiar short meter hymns are:

"Blest Be the Tie" (No. 256)
"Rise Up, O Men of God" (No. 268)
"Breathe on Me, Breath of God" (No. 317)
Its rhyme is *abab*:

"Blest be the tie that binds	(6 syllables) a
Our hearts in Christian love;	(6 syllables) b
The fellowship of kindred minds	(8 syllables) a
Is like to that above."	(6 syllables) b

(No. 256)

or *abcb*:

"I love thy kingdom, Lord,	(6 syllables) a
The house of thine abode,	(6 syllables) b
The church our blest Redeemer saved	(8 syllables) c
With his own precious blood."	(6 syllables) b

(No. 240)

Chapter 9

THE ROLE OF THE LEADER IN CONGREGATIONAL SINGING

Most Southern Baptist churches are of the tradition which calls for the leader of congregational singing to select the hymn, determine the manner, mood, and tempo in which it is sung, and stand before the congregation to conduct the singing. He must do all those things on the basis of his own judgment. The charismatic quality of his leadership is difficult to define or communicate, but it is usually a vital element which affects congregational singing.

Charles M. Alexander, who lived from 1867 to 1920, was the first charismatic song leader to gain international fame. P. P. Bliss, Ira D. Sankey, James McGranahan, and Philip Phillips, were all well-known evangelistic song leaders in the last half of the nineteenth century, and were products of the rising tide of evangelism of that era. They were among the first in the vanguard of gospel song development, and they led great throngs of people, usually from the keyboard of a reed organ. Their strong voices provided the guiding sound for the people. Alexander was the first to stand before the audience and lead with his arms and hands. He first did so in a series of evangelistic meetings sponsored by D. L. Moody during the Chicago World's Fair in 1893. In the years that followed, Alexander was associated with such evangelists as M. B. Williams, R. A. Torrey, and J. Wilbur Chapman.

The phenomenon of the evangelistic song leader did not occur in isolation or develop unrelated to other influences. The rise of

Romanticism in the nineteenth century provided the climate for musical virtuosity to blossom to full flower. The star, the prima donna, the much-sought-after headliner appeared. The great singer, the great pianist, the great violinist, and their public and private lives became front-page copy for the press.

The appearance of the great conductors came toward the end of the nineteenth century. Antal Dorati points out that the old playbills in Venice, announcing the first performance of Verdi's *La Traviata* in 1853, carry no mention of the conductor.

The various contributors to the performances are listed in great detail: from the authors (the librettist first) through the protagonists, down to the wigmaker's assistant. Everyone's name is carried in full. Only one participant is conspicuously omitted . . . the conductor.[1]
Long before Verdi's death in 1901, the conductor had achieved star status, and was recognized as a hero in his own right.

Verdi was still alive when Charles M. Alexander, this charming young man from Maryville, Tennessee, began his career as an evangelistic song leader. Homer Rodeheaver and Cliff Barrows have followed in his tradition, and it is that tradition that has been accepted in most Southern Baptist churches. There are still quite a number of churches that are served by organist-choir directors who lead the choir and the congregational singing from the console of the organ.

Regardless of the style of leadership the local church chooses to provide, it is imperative that we discover new ways to increase audience participation of the congregation in hymn singing.

During the Convocation on Congregational Singing in Nashville, Tennessee, April 29-May 1, 1974, a workgroup of twenty-five ministers of music from fourteen states developed the following statements regarding the role of the leader in congregational singing.

1. We believe that the effectiveness of congregational singing is determined largely by the leader.

2. We believe that the effectiveness of this leader is determined largely by his ability to act and react in three basic areas.

    (1) Influencing the congregation:

        a. Spiritually—reflecting and magnifying the person of

---

[1]Antal Dorati, "What Is a Conductor?", *They Talk About Music* (Rockville Centre, N.Y: Belwin-Mills Publishing Corp., 1971), Vol. 1, p. 11.

Christ. This influence is generated largely as a result of the leader's contact with the people in roles other than that of the congregational song leader. Yet, his acceptance as a music leader is influenced by his acceptance as a person by the congregation.

    b. Physically—by presenting a convincing and confident appearance.

    c. Musically—through adequate educational preparation and experience.

       (a) He should have a thorough knowledge of hymnic literature—historically, theologically, and musically.

       (b) He should skillfully determine the judgments relative to the hymn singing.

       (c) He should determine the needed accompaniment and the manner in which it should be used.

    d. Psychologically

       (a) Projecting a positive attitude.

       (b) Eliciting a positive response from the congregation.

       (c) Maintaining a consensus of approval from the congregation.

(2) Exhibiting a sensitivity to the expressed needs of the congregation:

    a. Spiritually—by an awareness of previous spiritual experiences of the members of the congregation.

    b. Intelligently—by knowing the cultural and educational climate of the congregation.

    c. Musically—by knowing the musical talent and experience within the congregation.

    d. Psychologically—by being aware of the psychological responses of the congregation.

(3) Developing and using resources and creative techniques for effective congregational singing:

    a. He must determine methods and techniques that he can use effectively within the limitations of his own personality and ability.

    b. His methods and techniques should be well planned rather than extemporaneous in character.

While we speak positively concerning the role of the leader of congregational singing, the personal characteristics, musical talents, vocal capabilities, conducting skills, etc., that are most desirable are somewhat difficult to describe. The individual's personal appearance before the congregation is important. His musical talents will be apparent to the congregation. The confidence with which he sings as he directs the hymns will surely be noticeable. The manner in which he conducts will reveal ease of gesture or awkardness and inexperience. Yet, there are successful leaders of congregational singing who do not possess in abundance all of these qualifications. Through some charismatic appeal the congregation responds enthusiastically and the singing goes on.

It seems that there are a few basic factors that may be observed in a successful leader of congregational singing that might be identified.

1. *A love of singing.* If the person leading the singing thoroughly enjoys this experience, that enjoyment will be contagious and will inspire persons in the congregation to want to sing.

2. *A pleasant singing voice.* The sound of the voice should be sure and confident. The congregation will respond positively or negatively, to the singer's voice.

3. *A confident manner of leading.* This factor speaks to the leader being perfectly at ease all through the singing of the hymn—at the opening phrase, at the end of the stanzas, and at the beginning of each subsequent stanza. He must establish a comfortable tempo and pace for the hymn that is appropriate for the congregation.

These three factors seem to be fundamental. Other characteristics or elements involved in this experience add to the dimension of leadership if they are positive. The motion of hand and arm in the traditional patterns of duple, triple, and quadruple meter can be helpful, but they are not imperative. To master the graceful motions of those patterns by no means guarantees that the person automatically becomes a skilled and qualified congregational song leader.

Since the hymnal is the basic tool of the leader of congregational singing, it must become an object of intense and continued study. It is imperative for the leader to know the subject matter of the texts, and to be able to sing the tunes. Unfamiliar tunes should be learned and practiced until they can be sung and led confidently.

The joy of leading persons in hymn singing is a blessed opportunity and a responsibility that presents a serious challenge to the church musician interested in effective service.

APPENDIX 1

Free Organ Accompaniments

Cassler, G. Winston, *Organ Descants for Selected Hymn Tunes* (Augsburg)

Coleman, Henry, *Varied Hymn Accompaniments* (Oxford)

Herbek, Raymond, *Organ Accompaniments for Congregational Singing* (Broadman)

Johnson, David N., *Free Harmonizations of Twelve Hymn Tunes* (Augsburg)

Johnson, David N., *Free Hymn Accompaniments for Manuals, Books 1 and 2* (Augsburg)

Jones, Jack, *Come, Christians, Join to Sing* (Broadman)

Jordan, Alice, *Hymns of Grateful Praise* (Broadman)

Lowe, David, *Praise to the Lord, the Almighty* (Broadman)

MacDonald, Robert, *Organ-Piano Accompaniments for Congregational Singing* (Broadman)

Thiman, Eric, *Varied Accompaniments to 34 Hymns* (Oxford)

Wood, Dale, *New Settings of Twenty Well-Known Hymntunes* (Augsburg)

Suggested Tempos for Hymns in *Baptist Hymnal,* 1975

This list provides for each title in *Baptist Hymnal* a suggested tempo range for each hymn. Unless otherwise indicated, the beat note is assumed to be a quarter note. If the indicated range is, for example, 80-88, this means that an appropriate tempo would be between 80 and 88 quarter notes per minute.

A Charge to Keep I Have, 407 (108-116)
A Mighty Fortress Is Our God, 37 (72-88)
Abide with Me, 217 (80-92)
Alas, and Did My Savior Bleed, 113 (80-92)
All Creatures of Our God and King, 9 (♩ =80-92)
All for Jesus, All for Jesus, 485 (76-88)
All Glory, Laud, and Honor, 39 (84-100)
All Hail the Power of Jesus' Name (CORONATION), 40 (92-104)
All Hail the Power of Jesus' Name (DIADEM), 41 (84-96)
All Hail the Power of Jesus' Name (MILES LANE), 42 (88-100)
All People That on Earth Do Dwell, 17 (80-96)
All Praise to Thee, 43 (96-108)
All That Thrills My Soul, 434 (76-88)
All the Way My Savior Leads Me, 214 (80-92)
All to Thee, 346 (60-72)
Alleluia, 422 (60-72)
Alleluia! Alleluia!, 117 (100-112)
Am I a Soldier of the Cross, 388 (88-100)
Amazing Grace! How Sweet the Sound, 165 (80-96)
America, the Beautiful, 508 (84-100)
Angels, from the Realms of Glory, 87 (88-100)
Angels We Have Heard on High, 95 (100-112)
Are You Washed in the Blood, 162 (96-108)
As Jacob with Travel Was Weary One Day, 421 (♩ =84-96)
As We Gather Around the Table of Our Lord, 251 (76-88)
Ask Ye What Great Thing I Know, 60 (88-100)
At Calvary, 166 (80-96)
At the Cross, 157 (80-92)

At the Name of Jesus, 363 (84-96)
Awake, Awake to Love and Work, 413 (92-100)
Awake, My Soul, Awake, My Tongue, 96 (84-96)
Away in a Manger, 80 (76-88)
Be Thou My Vision, 212 (96-108)
Because He Lives, 448 (108-120)
Because I Have Been Given Much, 414 ($\textstyle\quad =60\text{-}72$)
Beneath the Cross of Jesus, 360 (80-92)
Blessed Assurance, Jesus Is Mine, 334 ($\textstyle\quad =66\text{-}76$)
Blessed Be the Name, 50 (84-96)
Blessed Redeemer, 109 ($\textstyle\quad =50\text{-}60$)
Blessed Savior, Thee I Love, 427 (84-96)
Blest Be the Tie, 256 (84-96)
Break Thou the Bread of Life, 138 (82-96)
Breathe on Me, 131 (96-108)
Breathe on Me, Breath of God, 317 (92-100)
Brethren, We Have Met to Worship, 260 (88-100)
Built on the Rock the Church Doth Stand, 235 (92-104)
By and By, 506 (88-100)
Child in the Manger, 84 (120-138)
Children of the Heavenly Father, 207 (63-72)
Christ Is the World's True Light, 274 (84-96)
Christ Receiveth Sinful Men, 167 (80-92)
Christ the Lord Is Risen Today, 114 (88-100)
Christian Hearts, in Love United, 253 (80-92)
Christian Men, Arise and Give, 141 (92-100)
Come, All Christians, Be Committed, 362 ($\textstyle\quad =72\text{-}84$)
Come, Christians, Join to Sing, 61 (104-116)
Come, Come, Ye Saints, 210 (66-80)
Come, Holy Spirit, Dove Divine, 242 (92-104)
Come, Holy Spirit, Heavenly Dove, 134 (76-88)
Come, Let Us Join Our Cheerful Songs, 126 (80-92)
Come, Thou Almighty King, 2 (92-104)
Come, Thou Fount of Every Blessing (NETTLETON), 13 (66-80)
Come, Thou Fount of Every Blessing (WARRENTON), 12 (80-96)
Come, Thou Long-Expected Jesus, 79 (92-104)
Come, Ye Disconsolate, 211 (76-88)
Come, Ye Sinners, Poor and Needy (ARISE), 197 (80-92)
Come, Ye Sinners, Poor and Needy (BEACH SPRING), 196 (72-84)
Come, Ye Thankful People, Come, 233 (80-92)
Comfort, Comfort Ye My People, 77 (72-84)
Count Your Blessings, 231 (80-96)
Crown Him with Many Crowns, 52 (84-96)
Day by Day and with Each Passing Moment, 222 (80-88)
Day of Judgment! Day of Wonders!, 502 (84-96)

Dear Lord and Father of Mankind, 270 (76-88)
Declare, O Heavens, the Lord of Space, 47 ($\downarrow$ =80-92)
Do You Really Care?, 316 (84-96)
Down at the Cross, 454 (92-100)
Draw Thou My Soul, O Christ, 307 (84-96)
Face to Face with Christ My Savior, 489 (72-88)
Fairest Lord Jesus, 48 (76-92)
Faith Is the Victory, 377 ($\downarrow$. =60-72)
Faith of Our Fathers, 143 (88-100)
Fight the Good Fight, 394 (92-108)
Fill Thou My Life, O Lord My God, 460 (92-104)
Follow On, 226 (80-92)
Footsteps of Jesus, 325 (84-96)
For All the Saints, 144 (88-100)
For Me, 110 (80-92)
For the Beauty of the Earth, 54 (84-96)
For the Beauty of the Earth, 49 (84-96)
Forward Through the Ages, 146 (92-100)
Free from the Law, O Happy Condition, 168 ($\downarrow$. =60-72)
Free to Be Me, 331 (100-108)
From Every Race, from Every Clime, 247 (76-84)
Give Me the Wings of Faith, 498 (76-84)
Give to the Lord, As He Has Blessed You, 415 (84-96)
Give to the Winds Your Fears, 224 (80-92)
Glorious Is Thy Name, 59 (84-96)
Glorious Is Thy Name Most Holy, 419 (88-100)
Glory Be to God on High, 104 (92-100)
Glory Be to the Father, 4 (88-100)
Glory Be to the Father, 5 (88-96)
Go, Tell It on the Mountain, 82 (92-100)
Go to Dark Gethsemane, 112 (84-96)
God Be with You, 261 (84-92)
God, Give Us Christian Homes, 397 (92-100)
God Himself Is with Us, 16 (96-108)
God Is Love, His Mercy Brightens, 36 (80-92)
God Is My Strong Salvation, 343 (112-120)
God Is Working His Purpose Out, 509 (104-116)
God Loved the World So That He Gave, 445 (96-104)
God Moves in a Mysterious Way, 439 (80-92)
God of Earth and Outer Space, 20 (80-92)
God of Grace and God of Glory, 265 (80-92)
God of Mercy, God of Grace, 297 (104-112)
God of Our Fathers, 149 (92-104)
God, Our Father, We Adore Thee, 3 (92-104)
God, Who Stretched the Spangled Heavens, 150 (92-104)

God Will Take Care of You, 219 (♪ =120-132)
God's World Today, 359 (80-92)
Good Christian Men, Rejoice, 90 (72-84)
Good Christian Men, Rejoice and Sing, 123 (104-112)
Grace Greater than Our Sin, 164 (92-104)
Great Is Thy Faithfulness, 216 (92-104)
Great Redeemer, We Adore Thee, 51 (100-112)
Guide Me, O Thou Great Jehovah, 202 (92-104)
Hark! The Herald Angels Sing, 83 (100-112)
Have Faith in God, 376 (84-96)
Have No Fear, Little Flock, 225 (69-76)
Have Thine Own Way, Lord, 349 (92-104)
He Hideth My Soul, 451 (104-112)
He Included Me, 170 (♩. =56-66)
He Is Able to Deliver Thee, 479 (92-104)
He Is So Precious to Me, 449 (104-112)
He Keeps Me Singing, 435 (84-96)
He Leadeth Me! O Blessed Thought, 218 (92-104)
He Lives, 438 (♩. =72-84)
He Who Would Valiant Be, 384 (92-104)
Heaven Came Down, 425 (♩. =60-69)
Heavenly Sunlight, 472 (♩. =72-80)
Here at Thy Table, Lord, 246 (♩ =58-66)
Here Is My Life, 356 (76-84)
He's Everything to Me, 463 (80-92)
Higher Ground, 324 (80-92)
His Gentle Look, 318 (76-88)
His Name Is Wonderful, 71 (80-92)
Holy Bible, Book Divine, 139 (100-112)
Holy, Holy, Holy, 1 (80-92)
Holy Spirit, Light Divine, 135 (92-104)
Hope of the World, 364 (92-104)
How Firm a Foundation, 383 (♩ =60-72)
How Gracious Are Thy Mercies, Lord, 230 (92-104)
How Great Thou Art, 35 (72-84)
How Sweet the Name of Jesus Sounds, 464 (92-104)
I Am His, and He Is Mine, 342 (♩ =72-80)
I Am Not Skilled to Understand, 433 (80-92)
I Am Resolved, 177 (92-104)
I Am Thine, O Lord, 352 (92-104)
I Bless the Christ of God, 286 (84-96)
I Gave My Life for Thee, 417 (♪=52-60)
I Have Decided to Follow Jesus, 191 (72-80)
I Hear Thy Welcome Voice, 175 (72-84)
I Know Not What the Future, 492 (80-92)

I Know that My Redeemer Lives, 436 (♩ =72-80)
I Know that My Redeemer Liveth, 122 (92-104)
I Know Whom I Have Believed, 344 (104-116)
I Love Thee, 75 (80-92)
I Love Thy Kingdom, Lord, 240 (80-92)
I Love to Tell the Story, 461 (92-104)
I Need Thee Every Hour, 379 (72-84)
I Saw the Cross of Jesus, 483 (80-92)
I Sing the Almighty Power of God, 154 (92-104)
I Stand Amazed in the Presence, 63 (84-96)
I Surrender All, 347 (72-84)
I Waited for the Lord My God, 402 (84-96)
I Will Not Be Afraid, 452 (72-84)
I Will Sing of My Redeemer, 465 (♩.=72-84)
I Will Sing the Wondrous Story, 53 (84-96)
I Will Sing the Wondrous Story, 55 (84-96)
If You Will Only Let God Guide You, 203 (80-92)
I'll Live for Him, 189 (84-92)
I'm Not Ashamed to Own My Lord, 450 (84-96)
Immortal, Invisible, God Only Wise, 32 (84-96)
Immortal Love, Forever Full, 329 (72-84)
In Christ There Is No East or West, 258 (80-92)
In Heavenly Love Abiding, 204 (92-104)
In Loving-Kindness Jesus Came, 426 (72-80)
In Memory of the Savior's Love, 249 (80-92)
In the Cross of Christ I Glory, 70 (92-104)
In the Garden, 428 (♪=84-104)
In Times Like These, 469 (63-72)
Infant Holy, Infant Lowly, 94 (80-92)
It Came upon the Midnight Clear, 86 (♩.=60-72)
It Is Well with My Soul, 339 (80-92)
It's So Wonderful, 467 (88-96)
I've Found a Friend, O Such a Friend, 423 (72-80)
I've Got Peace Like a River, 458 (90-104)
Jerusalem, My Happy Home, 488 (♩.=69-80)
Jesus Calls Us o'er the Tumult, 367 (84-96)
Jesus Christ Is Risen Today, 115 (92-104)
Jesus, Friend of Thronging Pilgrims, 100 (84-96)
Jesus Is All the World to Me, 424 (♩. =60-69)
Jesus Is Lord of All, 353 (100-112)
Jesus Is Tenderly Calling, 188 (♩.=52-60)
Jesus, Keep Me Near the Cross, 351 (♪=92-100)
Jesus Lives and Jesus Leads, 38 (84-96)
Jesus, Lover of My Soul, 172 (92-100)
Jesus Loves Me, 336 (92-100)

Jesus Makes My Heart Rejoice, 386 (84-96)
Jesus! Name of Wondrous Love, 74 (84-96)
Jesus Paid It All, 156 (72-80)
Jesus Shall Reign Where'er the Sun, 282 (♩ =69-80)
Jesus, Still Lead On, 500 (80-92)
Jesus, the Very Thought of Thee, 73 (84-96)
Jesus, Thou Joy of Loving Hearts, 72 (96-104)
Jesus, Thy Boundless Love to Me, 326 (96-104)
Jesus! What a Friend for Sinners, 64 (84-96)
Jesus, with Thy Church Abide, 241 (96-104)
Joy to the World! The Lord Is Come, 88 (96-108)
Joyful, Joyful, We Adore Thee, 31 (96-108)
Just a Closer Walk with Thee, 481 (58-66)
Just As I Am, 187 (72-80)
Just As I Am, 186 (72-80)
Just As I Am, Thine Own to Be, 243 (84-90)
Just When I Need Him Most, 220 (♩. =72-80)
Lead Me to Calvary, 350 (84-96)
Lead On, O King Eternal, 420 (100-108)
Leaning on the Everlasting Arms, 254 (96-104)
Let All the World in Every Corner Sing, 24 (92-100)
Let Jesus Come into Your Heart, 179 (♩. =56-66)
Let Others See Jesus in You, 294 (♩. =48-56)
Let the Song Go Round the Earth, 306 (96-104)
Let Us Break Bread Together, 252 (92-100)
Let Us with a Gladsome Mind, 27 (96-108)
Like a River Glorious, 208 (♩ =69-80)
Living for Jesus, 348 (96-104)
Look, Ye Saints! The Sight Is Glorious, 121 (♩ =76-84)
Lord, I Want to Be a Christian, 322 (80-92)
Lord, I'm Coming Home, 174 (60-72)
Lord, Lay Some Soul upon My Heart, 298 (96-104)
Lord of Our Life, 145 (88-96)
Lord, Send a Revival, 272 (♩ =48-56)
Lord, Speak to Me, that I May Speak, 276 (80-92)
Lord, Who Dost Give to Thy Church, 239 (108-116)
Lord, You Bid Us Ever, 378 (88-96)
Love Divine, All Loves Excelling, 58 (88-96)
Love Is the Theme, 453 (100-112)
Love Lifted Me, 462 (60-72)
Low in the Grave He Lay, 118 (76-88)
Majestic Sweetness Sits Enthroned, 267 (108-116)
Make Me a Blessing, 290 (120-132)
Make Me a Channel of Blessing, 262 (52-63)
Make Room Within My Heart, O God, 321 (92-100)

"Man of Sorrows," What a Name, 56 (80-92)
May the Mind of Christ My Savior, 328 (80-92)
Mine Eyes Have Seen the Glory, 510 (76-88)
Moment by Moment, 381 (92-100)
More About Jesus, 327 ($\downarrow$. $=52$-63)
More Love to Thee, O Christ, 484 (84-92)
Morning Has Broken, 151 ($\downarrow$.$=48$-60)
Must Jesus Bear the Cross Alone, 494 (92-100)
My Blessed Savior, Is Thy Love, 431 (88-100)
My Country, 'Tis of Thee, 511 (88-96)
My Faith Has Found a Resting Place, 380 (84-96)
My Faith Looks Up to Thee, 382 (84-96)
My God, I Love Thee, 57 (92-100)
My God Is There, Controlling, 153 (72-80)
My Heart Looks in Faith, 332 (96-108)
My Jesus, I Love Thee, 76 (84-96)
My Lord Is Near Me All the Time, 209 (84-96)
My Master Was So Very Poor, 103 (84-92)
My Singing Is a Prayer, 412 (92-100)
My Song Is Love Unknown, 486 (100-112)
My Soul in Sad Exile, 338 (96-108)
Near to the Heart of God, 354 (84-96)
Nearer, My God, to Thee, 333 (80-92)
New Born Again, 474 (80-92)
New Life for You, 299 (92-104)
No, Not Despairingly, 173 (84-96)
No, Not One, 478 (76-84)
Nothing but the Blood, 158 (96-104)
Now I Belong to Jesus, 477 (84-96)
Now Thank We All Our God, 234 (76-88)
O Breath of Life, 137 (66-76)
O Church of God, Triumphant, 237 (88-100)
O Come, All Ye Faithful, 81 (96-108)
O Come, Loud Anthems Let Us Sing, 21 (80-92)
O Come, O Come, Emmanuel, 78 (100-108)
O for a Faith That Will Not Shrink, 390 ($\downarrow$ $=80$-92)
O for a Thousand Tongues to Sing, 69 (80-92)
O God in Heaven, Whose Loving Plan, 396 (92-100)
O God of Every Time and Place, 320 ($\downarrow$ $=60$-72)
O God of Our Fathers, 507 (92-100)
O God, Our Help in Ages Past, 223 (76-84)
O God, We Pray for All Mankind, 305 (96-108)
O God, Who to a Loyal Home, 398 (72-84)
O Gracious Lord, Accept Our Praise, 19 (92-100)
O Happy Day That Fixed My Choice, 457 ($\downarrow$ $=72$-80)

O Jesus, I Have Promised, 365 (88-96)
O Little Town of Bethlehem, 85 (84-100)
O Lord, Who Came to Earth to Show, 309 (96-104)
O Love of God Most Full, 482 (96-104)
O Love That Wilt Not Let Me Go, 368 (80-88)
O Master, Let Me Walk with Thee, 369 (108-116)
O My Soul, Bless God the Father, 34 (80-92)
O Perfect Love, 395 (88-100)
O Sacred Head, Now Wounded, 105 (80-88)
O Sing a Song of Bethlehem, 99 (108-116)
O Spirit of the Living God, 264 (90-102)
O Teacher, Master of the Skill, 443 (90-102)
O That Will Be Glory, 497 (126-138)
O the Deep, Deep Love of Jesus, 340 (72-84)
O Thou, in Whose Presence, 372 (♩ =60-66)
O Thou to Whose All-Searching Sight, 470 (♩ =69-76)
O Word of God Incarnate, 140 (88-100)
O Worship the King, 30 (96-108)
O Zion, Haste, 295 (96-112)
Of the Father's Love Begotten, 62 (♪ =108-120)
On Jordan's Stormy Banks, 490 (92-100)
Once to Every Man and Nation, 385 (72-84)
One Day, 127 (♩. =60-66)
One World, One Lord, One Witness, 296 (♩ =72-80)
Only Trust Him, 183 (80-92)
Onward, Christian Soldiers, 393 (84-96)
Open My Eyes that I May See, 358 (♩. =56-66)
Our Father God, Thy Name We Praise, 206 (80-92)
Our Hope Is in the Living God, 201 (84-96)
Out of My Bondage, Sorrow, and Night, 178 (88-100)
Pass It On, 287 (108-120)
Pass Me Not, O Gentle Savior, 176 (80-92)
Peace in Our Time, O Lord, 310 (69-76)
Pentecostal Power, 130 (100-108)
People to People, 308 (92-100)
Praise God from Whom All Blessings Flow, 6 (80-92)
Praise God from Whom All Blessings Flow, 7 (100-108)
Praise Him, O Praise Him, 18 (92-100)
Praise Him! Praise Him!, 67 (♩. =72-84)
Praise, My Soul, the King of Heaven, 8 (100-108)
Praise the Lord, 14 (100-108)
Praise the Lord, the King of Glory, 46 (100-108)
Praise the Lord Who Reigns Above, 23 (100-108)
Praise the Lord! Ye Heavens, Adore Him, 11 (84-96)
Praise to the Lord, the Almighty, 10 (88-100)

Spirit of God, Descend upon My Heart, 132 (♩ =60-72)
Spirit of God, Our Comforter, 133 (84-96)
Spirit of the Living God, 136 (84-96)
Spread, O Spread the Mighty Word, 284 (92-100)
Stand Up and Bless the Lord, 26 (84-96)
Stand Up, Stand Up for Jesus, 389 (96-108)
Stand Up, Stand Up for Jesus, 391 (96-108)
Standing on the Promises, 335 (96-108)
Stir Thy Church, O God, Our Father, 269 (92-100)
Strong, Righteous Man of Galilee, 101 (84-96)
Sunshine in My Soul, 447 (84-96)
Surely Goodness and Mercy, 228 (92-100)
Sweet Hour of Prayer, 401 (92-100)
Sweet, Sweet Spirit, 255 (84-96)
Take My Life, and Let It Be, 373 (88-96)
Take My Life, and Let It Be, 374 (♩ =56-66)
Take My Life, Lead Me, Lord, 366 (80-92)
Take the Name of Jesus with You, 473 (88-96)
Take Up Thy Cross, 370 (92-100)
Teach Me, O Lord, I Pray, 406 (84-96)
Teach Me, O Lord, to Care, 312 (60-72)
Teach Me Thy Way, O Lord, 330 (96-104)
Teach Me to Pray, 399 (♩.=48-60)
Tell It Out with Gladness, 275 (96-108)
Tell It to Jesus, 404 (84-96)
Tell Me the Story of Jesus, 437 (76-84)
Tell the Good News, 288 (84-96)
Thank the Lord with Joyful Heart, 466 (88-100)
The Banner of the Cross, 387 (84-96)
The Bond of Love, 259 (66-76)
The Bread of Life for All Men Broken, 250 (88-96)
The Cattle on a Thousand Hills, 152 (84-96)
The Church's One Foundation, 236 (88-100)
The First Lord's Day, 119 (92-100)
The First Noel the Angel Did Say, 91 (96-108)
The God of Abraham Praise, 25 (88-100)
The Great Physician, 102 (♩.=56-66)
The Head That Once Was Crowned, 125 (84-96)
The King of Love My Shepherd Is, 215 (72-84)
The Lily of the Valley, 459 (72-84)
The Lord Will Come, 128 (84-96)
The Lord's My Shepherd, 341 (72-84)
The Nail-Scarred Hand, 192 (72-80)
The Old Rugged Cross, 430 (♪=72-84)
The Savior Is Waiting, 182 (76-84)

We're Marching to Zion, 505 (♩.=66-76)
Were You There, 108 (80-88)
We've a Story to Tell, 281 (84-96)
What a Friend We Have in Jesus, 403 (76-84)
What If It Were Today?, 129 (♩.=60-72)
What Wondrous Love Is This, 106 (♩ =63-72)
When All Thy Mercies, O My God, 468 (♩ =72-80)
When I Survey the Wondrous Cross, 111 (♩ =56-66)
When Morning Gilds the Skies, 44 (84-90)
When Stephen, Full of Power and Grace, 392 (♩ =63-72)
When the Church of Jesus, 319 (84-96)
When the Morning Comes, 499 (72-80)
When the Roll is Called Up Yonder, 503 (84-96)
When We All Get to Heaven, 491 (92-100)
When We Walk with the Lord, 409 (84-96)
Where Can We Find Thee, Lord, So Near, 245 (♩ =66-76)
Where Charity and Love Prevail, 257 (♪=108-120)
Where Cross the Crowded Ways of Life, 311 (96-108)
Where He Leads Me, 371 (66-76)
Wherever He Leads I'll Go, 361 (84-92)
While Shepherds Watched Their Flocks, 97 (84-96)
Whiter than Snow, 185 (84-92)
Who at My Door Is Standing, 181 (84-92)
"Whosoever" Meaneth Me, 169 (80-92)
"Whosoever Will", 184 (84-96)
Why Do I Sing About Jesus?, 429 (♩.=46-54)
Will You Come?, 199 (66-76)
Without Him, 200 (80-88)
Wonderful, Wonderful Jesus, 432 (♩.=48-56)
Wonderful Words of Life, 142 (♩.=48-56)
Word of God, Across the Ages, 148 (88-96)
Ye Christian Heralds!, 289 (♩ =66-76)
Ye Must Be Born Again, 180 (♩.=56-60)
Ye Servants of God, 292 (88-96)

Listing of Hymns in *Baptist Hymnal, 1975* by Keys

Key of C
    A Mighty Fortress Is Our God, 37
    At Calvary, 166
    Child in the Manger, 84
    Christ Is the World's True Light, 274
    Christ the Lord Is Risen Today, 114
    Come, Ye Disconsolate, 211
    Do You Really Care? 316
    Free to Be Me, 331
    God Be with You, 261
    Good Christian Men, Rejoice and Sing, 123
    Have Faith in God, 376
    He Leadeth Me! O Blessed Thought, 218
    I Know that My Redeemer Liveth, 122
    Jesus Is Tenderly Calling, 188
    Lead On, O King Eternal, 420
    Low in the Grave He Lay, 118
    Make Me a Blessing, 290
    Morning Has Broken, 151
    My Song Is Love Unknown, 486
    O God Our Help in Ages Past, 223
    Rejoice, the Lord Is King, 120
    Send a Great Revival, 271
    Serve the Lord with Gladness, 411
    Spirit of God, Descend upon My Heart, 132
    Spread, O Spread the Mighty Word, 284
    Strong, Righteous Man of Galilee, 101
    Sweet Hour of Prayer, 401
    There Is a Fountain, 107
    We Thank Thee That Thy Mandate, 410
    What If It Were Today? 129
    When We All Get to Heaven, 491
    "Whosoever Will," 184
Key of C minor
    Built on the Rock the Church Doth Stand, 235
    Jesus, Friend of Thronging Pilgrims, 100
    My Master Was So Very Poor, 103
    O Thou to Whose All-Searching Sight, 470

Key of Db
  All for Jesus, All for Jesus, 485
  Beneath the Cross of Jesus, 360
  I Have Decided to Follow Jesus, 191
  It Is Well with My Soul, 339
  Jesus Is Lord of All, 353
  Jesus Lives and Jesus Leads, 38
  Jesus! Name of Wondrous Love, 74
  Just When I Need Him Most, 220
  My Singing Is a Prayer, 412
  Near to the Heart of God, 354
  One Day, 127
  Savior, Like a Shepherd Lead Us, 213
  Take My Life, Lead Me, Lord, 366
  Teach Me, O Lord, I Pray, 406
  Teach Me to Pray, 399
Key of D
  As We Gather Around the Table, 251
  Blessed Assurance, Jesus Is Mine, 334
  Children of the Heavenly Father, 207
  Christ Receiveth Sinful Men, 167
  Come, Thou Fount of Every Blessing, 12
  Day of Judgment! Day of Wonders! 502
  Dear Lord and Father of Mankind, 270
  Glory Be to God on High, 104
  God Loved the World So That He Gave, 445
  He Hideth My Soul, 451
  Holy, Holy, Holy, 1
  How Sweet the Name of Jesus Sounds, 464
  I Am His, and He Is Mine, 342
  I Am Not Skilled to Understand, 433
  I Surrender All, 347
  Jesus, with Thy Church Abide, 241
  Joy to the World! The Lord Is Come, 88
  Let All the World in Every Corner Sing, 24
  Let the Song Go Round the Earth, 306
  O Church of God, Triumphant, 237
  O God of Our Fathers, 507
  O Thou, in Whose Presence, 372
  Pass It On, 287
  Praise Him, O Praise Him, 18
  Praise, My Soul, the King of Heaven, 8
  Praise the Lord, 14
  Savior, Teach Me Day by Day, 291
  Shall We Gather at the River, 496

Show, O Lord, Thy Blessed Face, 227
The First Nowell the Angel Did Say, 91
We Are Climbing Jacob's Ladder, 147
We Gather Together, 229
We Have Heard the Joyful Sound, 278
We Praise Thee, O God, Our Redeemer, 15
Where Can We Find Thee, Lord, So Near, 245

Key of D minor
At the Name of Jesus, 363
From Every Race, from Every Clime, 247
God of Earth and Outer Space, 20
I Know that My Redeemer Lives, 436
Lord of Our Life, 145
O God of Every Time and Place, 320
Peace in Our Time, O Lord, 310
   (Final cadence D)
Teach Me, O Lord, to Care, 312
The Bread of Life for All Men Broken, 250
There's a Song in the Air, 93
What Wondrous Love Is This, 106
When Stephen, Full of Power and Grace, 392
When the Church of Jesus, 319

Key of Eb
Abide with Me, 217
All Creatures of Our God and King, 9
At the Cross, 157
Be Thou My Vision, 212
Blessed Redeemer, 109
Break Thou the Bread of Life, 138
Breathe on Me, 131
Come, Holy Spirit, Dove Divine, 242
Come, Thou Fount of Every Blessing, 13
Count Your Blessings, 231
Crown Him with Many Crowns, 52
Day by Day, 222
Declare, O Heavens, the Lord of Space, 47
Fairest Lord Jesus, 48
Faith Is the Victory, 377
Footsteps of Jesus, 325
Forward Through the Ages, 146
Free from the Law, O Happy Condition, 168
Give to the Lord, As He Has Blessed You, 415
Give to the Winds Your Fears, 224
Glory Be to the Father, 5
Go to Dark Gethsemane, 112

God, Give Us Christian Homes, 397
God Moves in a Mysterious Way, 439
God of Our Fathers, 149
Great Is Thy Faithfulness, 216
Great Redeemer, We Adore Thee, 51
Have No Fear, Little Flock, 225
Have Thine Own Way, Lord, 349
Here at Thy Table, Lord, 246
Hope of the World, 364
I Hear Thy Welcome Voice, 175
I Know Not What the Future, 492
I Know Whom I Have Believed, 344
I Love Thee, 75
I Saw the Cross of Jesus, 483
I Waited for the Lord My God, 402
I Will Sing the Wondrous Story, 55
Immortal Love, Forever Full, 329
In Heavenly Love Abiding, 204
In Memory of the Savior's Love, 249
Jesus Loves Me, 336
Jesus Paid It All, 156
Jesus Shall Reign Where'er the Sun, 282
Jesus, Thou Joy of Loving Hearts, 72
Just As I Am, 186
Just As I Am, 187
Lead Me to Calvary, 350
Let Us Break Bread Together, 252
Lord, I Want to Be a Christian, 322
Lord, Who Dost Give to Thy Church, 239
May the Mind of Christ My Savior, 328
My Blessed Savior, Is Thy Love, 431
My Faith Looks Up to Thee, 382
My Lord Is Near Me All the Time, 209
No, Not Despairingly, 173
O Master, Let Me Walk with Thee, 369
O Perfect Love, 395
O Word of God Incarnate, 140
Of the Father's Love Begotten, 62
Onward, Christian Soldiers, 393
Our Father God, Thy Name We Praise, 206
Redeemed, 444
Satisfied, 345
Satisfied with Jesus, 455
Sing Praise to God Who Reigns Above, 22
Somebody's Knocking at Your Door, 480

Surely Goodness and Mercy, 228
Teach Me Thy Way, O Lord, 330
Tell Me the Story of Jesus, 437
The Church's One Foundation, 236
The Great Physician, 102
This Is My Father's World, 155
This Joyful Eastertide, 124
We Are Called to Be God's People, 405
We Praise Thee with Our Minds, O Lord, 45
Were You There, 108
We've a Story to Tell, 281
When the Morning Comes, 499
Ye Christian Heralds!, 289
Ye Must Be Born Again, 180

Key of E minor
God Is My Strong Salvation, 343
Here Is My Life, 356 (Refrain in G)
How Gracious Are Thy Mercies, Lord, 230
Make Room Within My Heart, O God, 321
(Final cadence E)
My God, I Love Thee, 57
O Come, O Come, Emmanuel, 78
O Sing a Song of Bethlehem, 99
O the Deep, Deep Love of Jesus, 340
Once to Every Man and Nation, 385
The God of Abraham Praise, 25
Thou, Whose Purpose Is to Kindle, 313
Where Charity and Love Prevail, 257

Key of F
All Praise to Thee, 43
All to Thee, 346
Am I a Soldier of the Cross, 388
Angels We Have Heard on High, 95
As Jacob with Travel, 421
Ask Ye What Great Thing I Know, 60
Awake, My Soul, Awake, My Tongue, 96
Away in a Manger, 80
Blest Be the Tie, 256
Breathe on Me, Breath of God, 317
By and By, 506
Come, All Christians, Be Committed, 362
Come, Holy Spirit, Heavenly Dove, 134
Come, Thou Almighty King, 2
Come, Thou Long-Expected Jesus, 79
Come, Ye Thankful People, Come, 233

Comfort, Comfort Ye My People, 77
Fill Thou My Life, O Lord My God, 460
For the Beauty of the Earth, 49
Give Me the Wings of Faith, 498
Glorious Is Thy Name, 59
God Himself Is with Us, 16
God, Who Stretched the Spangled Heavens, 150
God's World Today, 359
Good Christian Men, Rejoice, 90
Hark! The Herald Angels Sing, 83
He Who Would Valiant Be, 384
Heaven Came Down, 425
Heavenly Sunlight, 472

His Gentle Look, 318

His Name Is Wonderful, 71

Holy Bible, Book Divine, 139

I'll Live for Him, 189

I Love Thy Kingdom, Lord, 240

I Sing the Almighty Power of God, 154

I Will Sing the Wondrous Story, 53

Jerusalem, My Happy Home, 488

Jesus Christ Is Risen Today, 115

Jesus, Keep Me Near the Cross, 351

Jesus, Lover of My Soul, 172

Jesus, Thy Boundless Love to Me, 326

Jesus! What a Friend for Sinners, 64

Like a River Glorious, 208

Living for Jesus, 348

Lord, Lay Some Soul upon My Heart, 298

Lord, You Bid Us Ever, 378

Moment by Moment, 381

My Country, 'Tis of Thee, 511

My God Is There, Controlling, 153

My Jesus, I Love Thee, 76

No, Not One, 478

Now Thank We All Our God, 234

O Come, Loud Anthems Let Us Sing, 21

O for a Faith That Will Not Shrink, 390

O Gracious Lord, Accept Our Praise, 19

O Happy Day That Fixed My Choice, 457

O Little Town of Bethlehem, 85

O Lord, Who Came to Earth to Show, 309

O Love of God Most Full, 482

On Jordan's Stormy Banks, 490

Wonderful Words of Life, 142
Word of God, Across the Ages, 148
Key of F minor
    Awake, Awake to Love and Work 413
    God Is Working His Purpose Out, 509
      (Final cadence F)
    O God, Who to a Loyal Home, 398
Key of G
    All Hail the Power of Jesus' Name, 40
    All People That on Earth Do Dwell, 17
    All the Way My Savior Leads Me, 214
    Alleluia, 422
    Alleluia! Alleluia! 117
    Amazing Grace! How Sweet the Sound, 165
    Christian Hearts, in Love United, 253
    Christian Men, Arise and Give, 141
    Come, Come Ye Saints, 210
    Come, Ye Sinners, Poor and Needy, 196
    Draw Thou My Soul, O Christ, 307
    Faith of Our Fathers, 143
    Fight the Good Fight, 394
    Follow On, 226
    For All the Saints, 144
    For the Beauty of the Earth, 54
    Glorious Is Thy Name Most Holy, 419
    Go, Tell It on the Mountain, 82
    God Is Love, His Mercy Brightens, 36
    God of Grace and God of Glory, 265
    God of Mercy, God of Grace, 297
    Grace Greater than Our Sin, 164
    Guide Me, O Thou Great Jehovah, 202
    He Is So Precious to Me, 449
    Higher Ground, 324
    I'm Not Ashamed to Own My Lord, 450
    In Loving-Kindness Jesus Came, 426
    Infant Holy, Infant Lowly, 94
    It's So Wonderful, 467
    I've Got Peace Like a River, 458
    Jesus Makes My Heart Rejoice, 386
    Jesus, Still Lead On, 500
    Jesus, the Very Thought of Thee, 73
    Joyful, Joyful, We Adore Thee, 31
    Lord, Speak to Me, that I May Speak, 276
    More Love to Thee, O Christ, 484
    Nearer, My God, to Thee, 333

New Born Again, 474
Nothing but the Blood, 158
Now I Belong to Jesus, 477
O Jesus, I Have Promised, 365
O Jesus, I have Promised, 365
O My Soul, Bless God the Father, 34
O Spirit of the Living God, 264
O Teacher, Master of the Skill, 443
Only Trust Him, 183
Our Hope Is in the Living God, 201
People to People, 308
Praise God, from Whom All Blessings Flow, 6
Praise God, from Whom All Blessings Flow, 7
Praise Him! Praise Him! 67
Purer in Heart, O God, 323
Revive Us Again, 263
Room at the Cross, 194
Search Me, O God, 266
Send Me, O Lord, Send Me, 293
Send the Light, 304
Share His Love, 285
Since I Have Been Redeemed, 442
Sing to the Lord of Harvest, 232
Something for Thee, 418
Stand Up and Bless the Lord, 26
Sweet, Sweet Spirit, 255
Take My Life, and Let It Be, 374
Tell It to Jesus, 404
The Head That Once Was Crowned, 125
The King of Love My Shepherd Is, 215
The Lord Will Come, 128
The Time Is Now, 193
The Way of the Cross Leads Home, 161
There's a Land That Is Fairer than Day, 495
'Tis So Sweet to Trust in Jesus, 375
Trusting Jesus, 441
Victory in Jesus, 475
We Have Heard the Joyful Sound, 277
We Would See Jesus; Lo! His Star, 98
We're Marching to Zion, 505
When All Thy Mercies, O My God, 468
Ye Servants of God, 292

Key of G minor
    Come, Ye Sinners, Poor and Needy, 197
    If You Will Only Let God Guide You, 203

Open My Eyes that I May See, 358
Out of My Bondage, Sorrow, and Night, 178
Pass Me Not, O Gentle Savior, 176
Pentecostal Power, 130
Redeemed, How I Love to Proclaim It, 446
Rejoice, All Ye People, 116
Savior, Again to Thy Dear Name, 65
Since Jesus Came into My Heart, 487
Sing We the King, 493
Softly and Tenderly, 190
Soldiers of Christ, in Truth Arrayed, 315
Stand Up, Stand Up for Jesus, 391
Sunshine in My Soul, 447
Take the Name of Jesus with You, 473
Thank the Lord with Joyful Heart, 466
The Sheltering Rock, 195
The Star-Spangled Banner, 512
There Is a Name I Love to Hear, 66
To God Be the Glory, 33
We Believe in One True God, 29
We Bless the Name of Christ the Lord, 244
We Have a Gospel to Proclaim, 301
We Lift Our Hearts in Songs of Praise, 416
When the Roll Is Called Up Yonder, 503
Whiter than Snow, 185
"Whosoever" Meaneth Me, 169
Why Do I Sing About Jesus? 429
Wonderful, Wonderful Jesus, 432

Key of A
Glory Be to the Father, 4
O Breath of Life, 137
Thou, Whose Almighty Word, 303

Key of A minor
For Me, 110
O Sacred Head, Now Wounded, 105 (Final cadence C)
Prayer Is the Soul's Sincere Desire, 400 (Final cadence C)

Key of Bb
All Glory, Laud, and Honor, 39
All Hail the Power of Jesus' Name, 41
All Hail the Power of Jesus' Name, 42
All That Thrills My Soul, 434
America, the Beautiful, 508
Angels, from the Realms of Glory, 87
Come, Let Us Join Our Cheerful Songs, 126
Face to Face with Christ My Savior, 489

God, Our Father, We Adore Thee, 3
God Will Take Care of You, 219
He Included Me, 170
He Is Able to Deliver Thee, 479
He Lives, 438
He's Everything to Me, 463
Holy Spirit, Light Divine, 135
How Great Thou Art, 35
I Am Resolved, 177
I Bless the Christ of God, 286
I Gave My Life for Thee, 417
In Christ There Is No East or West, 258
In the Cross of Christ I Glory, 70
It Came Upon the Midnight Clear, 86
Just a Closer Walk with Thee, 481
Let Us with a Gladsome Mind, 27
Love Divine, All Loves Excelling, 58
Love Is the Theme, 453
Love Lifted Me, 462
"Man of Sorrows," What a Name, 56
Mine Eyes Have Seen the Glory, 510
O God in Heaven, Whose Loving Plan, 396
O Zion, Haste, 295
Rescue the Perishing, 283
Ring the Bells of Heaven, 300
Rock of Ages, Cleft for Me, 163
Saved, Saved!, 160
Silent Night, Holy Night, 89
So Let Our Lips and Lives Express, 456
Standing on the Promises, 335
Take Up Thy Cross, 370
The Banner of the Cross, 387
The Bond of Love, 259
The Old Rugged Cross, 430
The Savior's Wondrous Love, 476
There Is Power in the Blood, 159
There Shall Be Showers of Blessing, 273
There's a Glad New Song, 471
There's a Wideness in God's Mercy, 171
To Worship, Work, and Witness, 238
When Morning Gilds the Skies, 44
Where Cross the Crowded Ways of Life, 311

Personal Learning Activities

Chapter 1
1. What did Paul write to the church in Corinth about his singing? (1 Cor. 14:15)
2. What were Paul's instructions to the church at Colosse concerning the indwelling word of Christ? (Col. 3:16-17)
3. List several positive literary and musical values of hymns.

Chapter 2
1. What are the negative factors of a tempo that is too fast?
2. What are the negative factors of a tempo that is too slow?
3. List several types of hymn tunes.
4. Name one hymn with long phrases.
5. Name one hymn with short phrases.

Chapter 3
1. What is important about the way the instrument introduces the hymn tune before it is sung?
2. What is meant by "letting the organ breathe with the congregation"?
3. What style of piano playing is most beneficial for congregational singing?
4. Why should the music director plan carefully with the instrumentalists?

Chapter 4
1. What physical factors affect congregational singing?
2. Describe factors influencing the placement of the organ console.
3. Describe factors influencing the placement of the piano.
4. What is the desirable range of the reverberation factor for congregational singing?

Chapter 5
1. Discuss the significance of unity in the congregational service.
2. With regard to congregational singing, what should long-range planning include?

3. Name three hymns appropriate for Bible Study Week.
4. Name three hymns appropriate for Doctrinal Emphasis Week.
5. Name three hymns for Church Music emphasis.

Chapter 6

1. What judgments need to be made regarding texts of hymns to be used in the service?
2. What judgments need to be made regarding the hymn tunes to be used in the service?
3. What is a *fermata*?
4. What does *rubato* mean?

Chapter 7

1. Why is the teaching of a new hymn a musical problem?
2. Name two hymns unfamiliar to you and identify two tunes with which you are familiar that fit these texts.
3. How may Sunday School and Church Training department periods be used for teaching new hymns?
4. Explain how the choir can assist in teaching new hymns to the congregation.

Chapter 8

1. What is Common Meter?
2. What is Short Meter?
3. What is Long Meter?
4. What is the metrical form of the Doxology?
5. What is the metrical form of "Amazing Grace"?

Chapter 9

1. Who was Charles M. Alexander?
2. How does the music director influence the congregation spiritually, physically, musically, and psychologically in the congregational singing?

The Church Study Course

The Church Study Course is a Southern Baptist educational system consisting of short courses for adults and youth combined with a credit and recognition system. More than 500 courses are available in 23 subject areas. Credit is awarded for each course completed. These credits may be applied to one or more of the 100 plus diploma plans in the recognition system. Diplomas are available for most leadership positions as well as general diplomas for all Christians. These diplomas are the certification that a person has completed from 5 to 8 prescribed courses. Diploma requirements are given in the catalogs.

Complete details about the Church Study Course system, courses available, and diplomas offered may be found in a current copy of the *Church Study Course Catalog* and in the study course section of the *Church Materials Catalog*. Study course materials are available from Baptist Book Stores.

The Church Study Course system is sponsored by the Sunday School Board, Woman's Missionary Union, and Brotherhood Commission of the Southern Baptist Convention.

How to Request Credit for this Course

This book is the text for course number 10013 in the subject area: *"Church Music Leadership."* This course is designed for five hours of group study.

Credit for this course may be obtained in two ways:

1. Read the book and attend class sessions. (If you are absent from one or more sessions, complete the "Personal Learning Activities" for the material missed.)
2. Read the book and complete the "Personal Learning Activities." (Written work should be submitted to an appropriate church leader.)

A request for credit may be made on Form 725 "Church Study Course Enrollment/Credit Request" and sent to the Awards Office, Sunday School Board, 127 Ninth Avenue, North, Nashville, Tennessee 37234. The form on the following page may be used to request credit.

A record of your awards will be maintained by the Awards Office. Twice each year copies will be sent to churches for distribution to members.

CHURCH STUDY COURSE
ENROLLMENT/CREDIT REQUEST (FORM-725)

PERSONAL CSC NUMBER (If Known)

INSTRUCTIONS:

1. Please PRINT or TYPE.
2. COURSE CREDIT REQUEST—Requirements must be met. Use exact title.
3. ENROLLMENT IN DIPLOMA PLANS—Enter selected diploma title to enroll.
4. For additional information see the Church Study Course Catalog.
5. Duplicate additional forms as needed. Free forms are available from the Awards Office and State Conventions.

TYPE OF REQUEST: (Check all that apply)

- ☐ Course Credit
- ☐ Enrollment in Diploma Plan
- ☐ Address Change
- ☐ Name Change
- ☐ Church Change

CHURCH		REQUEST FOR
Church Name		Name (First, MI, Last) ☐ Mr. ☐ Mrs. ☐ Miss
Mailing Address		Street, Route, or P.O. Box
City, State, Zip Code		City, State, Zip Code

DATE OF BIRTH

Month	Day	Year

COURSE CREDIT REQUEST

Use exact title	
1.	
Use exact title	
2.	
Use exact title	
3.	
Use exact title	
4.	
Use exact title	
5.	

ENROLLMENT IN DIPLOMA PLANS

If you have not previously indicated a diploma(s) you wish to earn, or you are beginning work on a new one(s), select and enter the diploma title from the current Church Study Course Catalog. Select one that relates to your leadership responsibility or interest. When all requirements have been met, the diploma will be automatically mailed to your church. No charge will be made for enrollment or diplomas.

Title of diploma	Age group or area
1.	
Title of diploma	Age group or area
2.	

Signature of Pastor, Teacher, or Study Leader	Date

MAIL THIS REQUEST TO ➡

CHURCH STUDY COURSE AWARDS OFFICE
RESEARCH SERVICES DEPARTMENT
127 NINTH AVENUE, NORTH
NASHVILLE, TENNESSEE 37234

BSSB-725 (Rev. 5-82)